PRA[...]

Lo[...]

"*Love Sick* is a journey worth ce[...]

—Tim McLoughl[...], [...] of *Heart of the Old Country*

"Frances Kuffel nails the world of middle-age dating. She is very honest, strikingly so, and tells of her travails with wit and understanding. The book is a treat. She is one hell of a storyteller."

—Rob Fasano, Moth Grand Slam winner

Eating Ice Cream with My Dog

(Previously published as *Angry Fat Girls*)

"[Kuffel] chronicles nearly every aspect of her life (binges in bed, childhood taunts, depression, meds, sex, breakups, firings and failings). . . . It is ultimately and simply Kuffel's own unsparing story that makes [*Eating Ice Cream with My Dog*] a necessary read." —*Bitch*

"Kuffel's narrative of rededication is a skilled blend of insight . . . and emotion . . . that never flags in intimacy, honesty or compassion. With keen humor and disarming skill, Kuffel introduces readers to the most private moments of the five women, whose addictive relationships with food make regular nourishment a constant nightmare of temptation." —*Publishers Weekly*

"A wake-up call to anyone who believes that weight management is a quick and easy feat. It's not. And Kuffel's greatest gift is a blast of hopeful reality for any brave reader ready to take herself on and honestly face her own food and weight demons."

—Pamela Peeke, author of *Fight Fat After Forty*

continued . . .

"[*Eating Ice Cream with My Dog*] is about women, weight loss, body image and what we did and did not learn growing up fat, and why losing weight—and keeping it off—is so hard. This book is honest, true and very funny."

—Cheryl Peck, author of *Fat Girls and Lawn Chairs*

Passing for Thin

"Inspiring . . . brazenly intimate . . . offers a powerful rebuff to anyone who believes that people can't change."   —*USA Today*

"[Kuffel's] writing is as clear and sharp as broken glass . . . a glorious read."   —*The New York Times*

"A talented writer."   —*The Boston Globe*

"Empathy, candor and courage are abundant."

—*Entertainment Weekly*

"Rife with snappy anecdotes and mordant humor . . . as fascinating in its grotesque insight as in its inspirational uplift."

—*The A.V. Club*

"[A] riveting memoir . . . grim humor . . . A hilarious and insightful book."   —*Psychology Today*

BOOKS BY FRANCES KUFFEL

Passing for Thin
Eating Ice Cream with My Dog
Love Sick

LOVE SICK

Frances Kuffel

BERKLEY BOOKS, NEW YORK

THE BERKLEY PUBLISHING GROUP
Published by the Penguin Group
Penguin Group (USA) LLC
375 Hudson Street, New York, New York 10014

USA • Canada • UK • Ireland • Australia • New Zealand • India • South Africa • China

penguin.com

A Penguin Random House Company

This book is an original publication of The Berkley Publishing Group.

LOVE SICK

PUBLISHING HISTORY
Berkley trade paperback edition / June 2014

ISBN 978-0-425-24747-1

PRINTED IN THE UNITED STATES OF AMERICA

10 9 8 7 6 5 4 3 2 1

Cover design by Diana Kolsky
Cover art: cut heart © Susan Fox / Trevillion Images
Interior text design by Laura K. Corless

The names and identifying characteristics of some of the individuals depicted in this book
have been changed to protect their privacy.

Penguin is committed to publishing works of quality and integrity.
In that spirit, we are proud to offer this book to our readers;
however, the story, the experiences, and the words
are the author's alone.

To Tom Graves

Tu m'affida, o mio tesor.

One

Penguin couples spend their lives apart from
each other and meet once a year in late March,
after traveling as far as seventy miles inland—
on foot or sliding on their bellies—to reach
the breeding site.

April

We are in Santa Fe to find a ghost. It is also, as he and I had discussed in a wearying back-and-forth series of phone calls and emails, my audition as Dar's girlfriend and, seven thousand feet higher than where we started out in Phoenix, we were breathless in all the wrong ways. Instead of canoodling our ghost into rearranging the furniture, I slept fitfully as the television murmured and flickered through a marathon of *Sasuke*. In the end, our only haunting is that "Need You Now" is on every radio station between Santa Fe and Phoenix, which is annoying but also fitting as we sit in the car outside his house having the Talk.

It is becoming more and more obvious that men are oblivious to what Friends with Benefits can start for a woman.

"I love you," he begins. "We have a lot in common. You know, the whole lit thing, and dogs, and a general sort of outlook on stuff. But then again, there are things that are important to me that we don't have in common. I don't know whether it's best to be with someone with whom you have everything in common or not. I had a girlfriend like that once, but the minute she came to visit me, I knew it was all wrong . . .

"So I dunno. One thing is that you're not exactly easygoing. You don't always relax and go with the flow. I mean, you never know what could happen, I s'pose. I *could* wake up one day and be in love with you. But I'm not now and I don't want to do anything that would jeopardize our friendship. That means a lot to me. You know that, right?"

I blow my nose in answer. I want out of his car. I want to get into my car, which is parked in his garage, and I want to drive to my father's house, get on the plane to New York the next morning, retrieve my dog from my friends Ben and Jean and tell them what didn't happen and then hold a weepy funeral with the mostly faithful love of Daisy, an ill-behaved, too-smart-for-her-own-good yellow Labrador, in the solitude of the Bat Cave.* *Don't say anything*, one part of me warns. *Have some dignity.*

---

* My apartment, aka the Bat Cave, is a not-very-long rectangular studio apartment with windows looking into my neighbor's garden. I have a slice of sunlight for about forty-five minutes each morning that does not cut into the perpetual dusk. I have not infrequently left the house thinking I am wearing black tights only to discover they are navy blue halfway to my destination. It's easy to take naps there.

"Okay." I hiccup and open the door. "I guess that's that. I gotta go."

He hugs me good-bye, an awkward bear hug in which I pat his back as though consoling him.

I'm so sick of this bullshit, I think.

.　.　.

I should have known, I think as the Midwest skeins me away from Dar. I should have known when I was late meeting him in Phoenix for the drive to New Mexico. I should have known when I found myself biting my lips in an ugly frown against my grinding jaw, that I was too tense, too scared to be girlfriend material.

I had no excuse for not knowing how tension crippled anything soft and fluid in me because I know the difference between scared, solo tension and the tension you admit to and find is as shared and rare as a yellow crocus flowering in the snow.

March

"God, France, I'm so sorry I'm not going to be here," Grace calls in disappointment on a heavy and cold Sunday afternoon. I am about to leave on my book tour to Seattle and Portland and am excited to see so many people from my past. Grace and I had been good friends in college but we'd lost touch in the last twenty years. I'd looked for her on various networking sites with no success, but her curiosity was equal to mine and she had found me in a two-second Google search. All Grace had to do was email me and we spent most of a Saturday on the phone reestablishing a comfy, happy friendship.

"I have lots of friends and family in Seattle, so I have plenty to do," I say, "although I really wanted to go to the movies with you."

She sighs and is about to answer when there is a loud crash and cursing on her end of the line. I wait through some mumbling and then laughter. "Kevin just knocked over the trash," she says. "He comes over most Sundays and makes brunch for us. But first we have to pick up banana peels and plum pits."

"And eggshells—ick!" I hear him call.

It's been thirty years since I've heard Kevin's voice but I could pick it out of Monday morning rush hour. I hadn't even heard of his sister, Grace, when Kevin Willoughby and I were pals for about five minutes in high school drama club. He's two years older than I, had dimples you could bury nickels in, dazzling blue eyes, a lovely tenor and he was one the most popular boys in school. He was perpetually jolly and surrounded by people; I was fat, a depressed underachiever, someone who went through friendships like Kleenex. I admired him for being all those things I was not and wasn't surprised when he got bored with acting. He went off to date the cream of the Joni Mitchell clones and the funniest cheerleaders, take the coolest drugs and ski with the maniacs. We lapsed into jokey hallway hellos and the thrill of having him sign my yearbook.

The ironies are rife. Kevin, gay and closeted, was hiding behind what I should have been learning—how to talk to the opposite sex, going to the prom, falling in love for the first time.

But of course his story didn't end there. After graduating, he came out and cozied up to Jack Daniel's like the boyfriend high school never gave him. I'd gone on to college and more college, worked in publishing, wrote a book about my dramatic weight loss and then wrote another book about my more mundane regain. I know from Grace that he's in his fragile first year of sobriety and is starting beauty college; I'm a sometimes–adjunct professor but mostly walk dogs for a living.

So much for our halcyon days. Which is why I am dying to talk to him.

"Put that Kevin on the phone," I demand. "I need to talk to Kevin Willoughby."

"How the hell are you?"

I start to laugh.

"Not well, Kevin. Not well at all."

"What's wrong, darling?"

"I have new neighbors."

"Are they partiers? Complainers?"

"No. They're gay."

"Uh-huh," he says cautiously, letting me know he's waiting to see how this plays out.

"They have the garden my apartment looks out on. Summer's coming and last night they were listening to *Fiddler on the Roof*."

I can hear the hideousness dawn on him. "I see."

"It's going to get very . . . brunchy around here in a couple of months. I swear I'll call the cops if they have *Oklahoma!* with their mimosas."

Kevin has a laugh that is as dangerous and infectious as

bubonic plague. I hunch-run to the toilet before I wet my pants, and when we catch our breath, he wheezes, "Where have you been all my life, Frances Kuffel, and when does your plane land?"

• • •

By the time we head out to Kevin's favorite pho noodle shop on East Yesler Way, I am as tense as I would be a month later in Santa Fe.

There is a difference, however. In Santa Fe, I am tight with waiting, wondering, searching for the magic words or slant of light to fill Dar with that love he isn't sure he doesn't have for me, a double-negative that is too big to overcome.

Kevin and I, on the other hand, have sat on his small balcony discussing AA and the 12-step program for compulsive overeating I've not been attending lately, telling our drunkalogue and fatalogue stories with increasing glee, then a sharp *ritenuto* into the grim side of addiction, how we avoided everyone and everything in order to eat or drink alone, consuming so much that we passed out only to wake hours later to do the same thing again, our underlying convictions that we are pieces of shit and that addiction is both our punishment and solace. At several points along the way, each of us lost everything and learned nothing. I declared bankruptcy in my thirties because I couldn't pay the cost of takeout. He was fired from a glamorous, well-paying job. Drunkenly careless, he contracted HIV in his thirties; overburdening my body with fat and hormones,

I had emergency surgery to remove a thirty-six-pound ovarian cyst and my gallbladder in my thirties. At 336 pounds, I couldn't walk for more than ten minutes. He spent the first three days in rehab leaning heavily on a walker.

We discover that we have unknowingly dallied in each other's shit and I am shaking from the intensity of the second conversation we've had since high school. I'm not hoping I'll turn, eyes bright, and give him a private peek at how pretty I can be. I am not waiting for Kevin to realize anything about me.

He already knows. He's known for years without knowing me. And I am shaking and sweating because I want to dance or scream the loop-de-loop of a roller coaster.

I look up at the soft blue March Seattle day as we walk to my car. Daffodils are out and the pear trees are flowering. Across the street is an old white house that needs rose trellises and hanging pots of begonias.

"Just think what *we'd* do to that house," I say as I fish out my keys.

"I *know*," he says in that way that says he really does.

April

I should know that Dar's aloof tolerance is a deal breaker when I beg to make one dash into the St. Francis souvenir shop. I want to buy gifts for my friends who are taking care of my dog. They are Vatican II babies like me who revel in bloodied martyrs and swooning penitents. Such tchotchkes have no charm for Dar, and he's eager to move on to the art galleries where he can speak seriously with owners about the Mesa museum he volunteers at. I snatch Christmas ornaments of Francis of Assisi and primitive angels, hurrying, embarrassed, not wanting to waste Dar's time.

When Kevin and I went down to the piers a month earlier, he knelt to pose goofily with a photo of Ivar Haglund at Ivar's Acres of Clams and solemnly wrapped his arms around a scary arcade clown. He deliberated with me over crab-shaped salt and pepper shakers and pulled a stranger over to photograph us with a plaster fisherman, then dragged me to the Olde Curiosity Shoppe to visit his friends, the petrified remains of a dog and a human who seems to be screaming that Mount Rainier has erupted and swallowed her child.

If I'm honest—or later, when I begin to get honest—I am mystified by Dar's lack of schlock idolatry. He's too smart and too funny not to groove on jumping beans and Barack and Michelle Obama Day of the Dead figurines. After all, he'd laughed at the junk in the truck stop we gassed up at, modeled a baseball cap with a propeller on top and stuck a navy blue leather cowboy hat on me.

What happens in a truck stop, I am forced to conclude, stays in the truck stop.

* * *

I am hurt but determined to make the best of it. I breathe deeply for the first few days back in Brooklyn, walking dogs and taking too many pictures of tulips showing their Georgia O'Keeffe to the clement sunshine, but I can't stop thinking about my conversation with Dar. I laugh crookedly and add to my list of Wrong Things to Say When Saying It's Over:

I love you, but I'm not in love with you.*

It goes right up there with:

You would like her.†
Let's get married, but to other people, and then tell each other about it.

And

I owe you an amends for how I treated you when we were together.‡

I do like absurdity. In the end I tell myself I've come out ahead. Then I turn my attention to Dar and to what went, maybe, right.

---

* Pretty stale for a lit-boy like Dar.

† No, I wouldn't. Trust me on this.

‡ No. You owe me public self-flagellation. I do not mean this metaphorically.

· · ·

"I want to remember . . ." Dar says, pounding along to "Need You Now" somewhere near Gallup on our way back to Phoenix, and proceeds to rattle off meaningful moments in our thirty-six-hour trip to fine arts purgatory. A few days later I email him from Brooklyn with the precise list:

> *The smell of pines as we climbed east and up in elevation from Phoenix*
>
> *The pitcher of ice water with floating tangerine quarters in the lobby of our hotel*
>
> *The portrait of our ghost, Julia Staab, hanging over our very own fireplace, across from our very own four-poster bed*
>
> *The pony-hide armchair in the art gallery*
>
> *The ukulelist and his girlfriend, who sang an affectless "Oh, Susannah" (and their conversation about clawhammer music after)*
>
> *Ginger-pineapple juice*
>
> *My entrée of shrimp with a green chili and lemongrass sauce [that he preferred to his plato supremo]; my lavender ice cream [that he preferred to his crème brulée]*
>
> *The urn of Mexican cocoa in the hotel lobby (the best he'd had since living in Nicaragua)*
>
> *The massage with oil made of bergamot, lemon, lavender and rosemary*
>
> *The prayer wheel garden*

"Thank you, thank you, thank you," he wrote back. "I love that you remembered that for me."

"*Love?*" I screech to Kevin. He's taken to calling me a couple of times a week before he has breakfast and goes off to cosmetology school. We talk about living one day at a time and how much we want and don't know how to be happy-joyous-and-free, as well as about the chittering Vietnamese students who dyed his hair platinum one slow afternoon and my audition in Santa Fe. "He loves my memory but he doesn't love me?"

"That's exaggerating, Frances, darling. I know he loves you."

"Yeah, yeah, yeah," I singsong back at him. The rest of that sentence doesn't need finishing.

"If I'm not *easygoing*, why did I let him eat my dinner? Why did I smile and go study paintings while he talked to street musicians and gallery owners?"

"What do *you* want to remember from the trip?"

I'm stumped. I liked my shrimp and the lavender ice cream but an overeater has a hard time remembering tastes. A massage is a massage. The prayer wheels in the cool daffodil light will stay with me, though. "I liked the storm drain covers," I say. "They had the city's coat of arms on them."

"That's hilarious! Seattle has special drains, too."

"I know! I took pictures of them. They're walking squids or something, right?"

"I'm not sure. So if you liked the drains, what would he repeat back as the things *you* wouldn't want to forget?"

"Probably the same things he loved," I say. His mother gave him the trip for graduation—he had finished yet another bachelor's degree, this time in social work. He'd earned that trip. Having earned the trip, it became a star turn, the Lone Ranger joined by Tonto so that he'd have someone to talk to and be admired by.

"When you're . . . uncomfortable," Kevin says, either searching for words or trying not to offend me, "you get all, you know, arms crossed and frowny-eyed and your voice gets kinda high-pitched. Did you do that?"

"You mean diffident? You saw the pictures he took of me. I'd give the Phantom of the Opera a shot at homecoming prince."

"How much did you apologize?"

"For how I looked?"

"Partly. But for the waiter not bringing water on time or the cost of gas or for him ordering the wrong meal?"

"Or for him not burning CDs to play in the car? Yeah, that was my fault, too."

• • •

The words "you never know what could happen" are still so alive in me that I rattle off Dar's pleasures in the trip as that last shred of hope that I'm too smart to grasp at very often. Memory and sentiment have always been my province. I'm the one who has family stories from generations back, insists on holiday traditions and cried when the seam of a leather jewelry box my mother gave me forty years ago finally ripped. Maybe it's being adopted or maybe it's not having kids of my own, but I worry that my little pod of Kuffels will fade a little around the edges if one of us doesn't know how to make my grandmother's sugar cookies or that my great-great-grandfather died walking north from Andersonville when the Civil War ended.

All that remembering of other people's stories makes me a sometimes-brilliant gift-giver. Such talents can make me less than easygoing, I suppose, but they *are* talents, fonts of generosity. Exactly what woman is going to remember bergamot and rosemary when she buys massage oil for Dar? Who will send him a perfect bouquet of daisies for graduation and give him a cotton candy maker for Christmas?

Do I buy love?

There has been a succession of such gifts that are so apt that the only thing I can top them with is to go away and leave my friend/crush/lover alone to enjoy them. That solemn teddy bear we named Étienne, the Irish print of the crofter's cottage, the Grover Washington CD, the book of World War II maps . . . ?

Or do such gifts demand too much gratitude?

Dar may find me high-strung, but it's not like I email him every week or even call him every month or confide my loneliness, depression and agoraphobia in him. In fact, he turns me into an insouciant ingénue. I tend to forget to turn the oven on when he comes to dinner at my father's house and not be able to make up my mind as to what kind of cheese we should buy: Is this what being un-easygoing is?

Does he remember how we met, for God's sake?

August 2005

Because of the heat wave stretching from coast to coast that prohibited dogs from flying, I had to leave Daisy, my boon companion, with my brother in Montana when I was due to go back to New York. Daisy is not an easy dog, but she'd been my blessed bane for the past two years. She is ageist and racist, and highly suspicious of wheelchairs, canes, crutches and walkers. Walking the broad length of the Promenade at night, she will sniff out and want to take down the drunks, drug addicts and mentally disabled from four blocks away. She comments on these people in a manner not dissimilar to Sandra Bernhard. For the last two years, I'd spent a couple of hours every day in the dog run lobbing balls while she shrieked "throw-the-ball-throw-the-ball-throw-the-ball" in a voice that disintegrated glass.

Finding myself alone was disorienting. My bed was too big. If the buzzer went off, there was no torrent of protest. I didn't have dirt in my shoes and mud stains on my shorts. I cleaned my apartment and threw out bags of dog hair and grit and it didn't stack up again by suppertime. I was forced to find something to do as I watched the weather reports in Missoula, Minneapolis and New York, and I decided to take advantage of my bachelorettehood.

What better statement of liberation could I make, then, than posting on craigslist? In the two years I'd had Daisy, I had had one sort-of boyfriend. In the few months before I got her, I'd gone through a mildly slutty period, but in my momentary independence I went, shall we say, a little over the top.*

I could have paid for any number of useful things—teeth whitening, having my apartment painted, a plane ticket to Milan, taxes—with what I spent on corsets, high heels, push-up bras, hose and garter belts in the summer of 2005. I got some good use out of them and when, after three weeks of record high temperatures, Daisy was finally able to fly home, I had been paddled, whipped, flogged and fucked in a number of creatively organic and inorganic ways. I was down to one or two emails of interest from the original post. If I was going to finish this project, I'd have to find a way that didn't excite her wild defense of me. Anyway, I was losing interest. I like kink as much as the next girl, but I think it's kinkier to be ball-gagged by someone whose mother has asked me to pass the mashed potatoes.

One of those lingering emails was from Dar. He thought my posting was quirky and too literate not to respond to. We spoke and I had no opinion of this younger man with a rather flat voice but I agreed to meet him for a movie.

Which he slept through.

We must have found something to talk about over iced tea

---

* I know that one guy really liked me. Was it the gift of his riding crop that stanched further contact?

afterward. I remember finding out that he has an MFA in creative writing and was from the West, which was enough to invite him to dinner at my apartment that week.

He arrived in a state of extreme nervousness. Daisy took one look at him and started humping him, something she'd done once before, to a fireman. She broke some of the tension he carried with him but as soon as he peeled her off he turned to me and said, "I have to tell you something before we go any further."

I shivered a little at that.

"I'm a crack addict."

I cocked my head and sized him up again. "I didn't know white boys could be crackheads."

"I'm a criminal," he said.

"You're an addict." I shrugged my shoulders and went into the kitchen to fetch the chamomile iced tea he'd mentioned was his favorite. "So what? I'm an addict, too."

"Not to crack. It's not the same."

I handed him a glass and sat down at my computer to pull up a research file. "Sugar and cocaine both affect dopamine receptors. Tolerance grows for each. The two substances are cross-addictive. Do you want to know more?"

He gulped his tea and then took another long sip. "I can't believe you remember I love iced chamomile," he said.

• • •

The company Dar had been working for had thought it wise for them to part ways. His lease had run out and, at the time we met, he'd decided to head to a friend's beach house to go cold turkey. He was in the midst of saying good-bye to ten years' worth of friends. After meeting up with old pals, he took to dropping in; when he was through with his farewells, he asked to stay for a night before hopping a bus to Georgia.

He stayed for ten days. The studio portion of the Bat Cave is about 15 by 40 feet, barely room for a single occupant. Now there were three, and one of us didn't sleep. Except for forays to see his dealer, Dar worked frantically—downloading weird software, writing fragments of bopper poetry or base-crazy wisdom—on his laptop as I worked on a book. It was unaccountably comfortable, each of us in our own bubble of thought, emerging occasionally to share a good line, a website or a song. I gave him Frou Frou's "Let Go" and he gave me the Postal Service's "Clark Gable." I would set a salad or bowl of yogurt at his side and two hours later he'd realize he'd eaten it and loved it. At night he created an elaborate ritual of tucking Daisy and me into bed.

The problem, he explained, was that, high, he found it hard to get an erection.

"But you would if you could, right?" I asked him about twice a day.

And one evening I came in from walking Daisy and he was splayed along the couch like Manet's "Woman Reclining in Spanish Dress with Kitten."

Except there was no kitten and he wasn't dressed.

"So?" he said as I stood in the door and gaped. "Ready?"

"Uh," I stuttered.

"It's time. You want to do this, right? Let's do it."

I laughed as nervously as hair dancing over a flame. He stood up and walked over, unleashed Daisy, inspected the leash for a moment and then flung it into the kitchen behind us.

"So you don't want to."

I stuttered some more. "I do. I'm just . . . taken aback."

"Abashed, disconcerted, out of countenance . . ."

"Surprised will do."

I had never giggled, cried and come at the same time. That conjunction of silly orgasmic stars would happen once more in my life, the second and last time Dar fucked me and I made love to him. At least he was long-sober the last time. At least he got it up on a whim and at least he came.

Still. Twice in five years can make a girl kind of tense.

April

A couple of weeks after Dar loved the memories I'd saved for him, I ask him for music suggestions. Knowing we are now at a permanent impasse there cannot be a more stupid request I could make. Whenever one of my students goes through a breakup, I urge her to go out immediately and buy an album by an artist she did not listen to with her ex. "Cut your hair, take a juggling class, rearrange your furniture," I advise. "Do whatever you have to do to become a person he doesn't know anymore." It begins with replacing the music because all she needs to do is run into 3 Doors Down on her iPod to start a day-long crying jag.

I am obviously bored out of my mind to invite Christopher O'Riley playing Radiohead into my life. With a lump in my throat, I listen to one tune and respond that I like it, then go back to playing Farm Town on Facebook.

Dar slams back. "What do you mean, you 'like' it? I sent you a playlist of songs I love and you listen to one and you 'like' it. You know music is one of the most important things to me. I think you owe me more consideration than that."

I stare at the email, wondering what to say to make it right. I've gotten myself into one of those dumb arguments that is about one thing but is really about deeper matters of the heart, and although I started it, I'm pissed off at the fierceness of his response. I can listen to the song again, apologize and find something profound to say about it, or I can inform him that he's overreacting to my mistake in asking for music that would remind me of his loose-hipped dancing forever.

Which I tell him. I might be a thinner, happier person if I felt and expressed my anger at the moment it's roused, so this spat is important. This is progress. I have never argued with a man I loved.

In fifteen minutes, we descend into an email tug-of-war of I-told-you-how-I-felt versus that's-exactly-why-I-can't-listen-to-these-songs. By the time he circles back to my lack of going with the flow, I'm browbeaten. "Stop this," I snap. "Let's just *stop*."

I mean a full, complete halt to all proceedings, but having argued my point of view I'm too tired to emphasize that to Dar.

What I say to Kevin is, "What the fuck does he mean I don't 'go with the flow'? We met on craigslist, for God's sake. I was letting men *spank* me that summer. He'd lost his job and apartment and was ten thousand bucks in crack debt when I took him in and kicked him out at the right time. You know I really want to move to Seattle, right? I have a life there. I have you and Grace and a family the size of the Osmonds within 500 miles. What's here? I walk dogs. I have about four friends here, and the only ones I actually socialize with are Ben and Jean. There isn't room to turn around in the Bat Cave. But I can't make the decision because maybe I should move to Phoenix. I hate that city, but I could take care of Dad and see Dar on a regular basis. In the five years I've known him, we see each other a couple of times a year. All I do is wave good-bye."

"Shouldn't you say that to Dar?" Kevin asks mildly.

"I can't. It's been such a hard month already." I imitate Dar's voice: " 'I love you but I'm not in love with you; you're too stressful; I love the way your brain works; you don't take me or my interests seriously.' I feel like one of those felt bull's-eyes with Velcro arrows of Dar's statements all over me."

Besides, if I let him keep arguing our way back to that night in the car outside his house, he'd have to clarify what he meant by my lack of easygoingness and I'm not sure I want to hear it.

"You gotta disengage, Princess. Stop emailing him. Start saving your money and come back to Seattle. I'm lonely for you."

All the tears of rage and love coalesce around my vocal cords at that. I miss Kevin, too. As ready as I've been for the last couple years to massacre my Visa card and move to Arizona, I've never woken up every morning hoping he will call me that day or text me a picture of the tomato seedlings in his kitchen window. Kevin does that. Kevin's genius is for making me feel part of his life by sharing the small things in the day. Dar's genius is for making room to twit witticisms between final exams or full appointment rosters.

"If I ever get it together to move out there," I tell him, "can we have one night a month when we watch sad movies and cry until midnight?"

"No. We have other things to do."

I think of our stop in the International District on the way back to his house. He had to buy some fish to feed his three adolescent turtles.

"Maybe feeding neon tetras to Me, Myself and I will be catharsis enough," I say.

"Yes," he purrs in his speaking-to-a-kid-with-a-scraped-knee voice. "Only pretty fishies for my babies. It's so much fun to watch them snap them up."

It could be our version of a reality TV family: food, love and gore.

Two

It takes Galapagos tortoises forty years to go through puberty.

The most important love is first love.

Freud would say that my first love was my father, and there is something to that. Little girls say their fathers can do anything, but mine really could. He set my broken arm, fixed my doll furniture, made the best spaghetti sauce, built a nineteen-foot sailboat, knew which mushrooms were poisonous and missed a lot of dinners because in our town, he was the first doc called for an emergency. My mother didn't know how to work the Magnavox stereo but I did because my dad and I listened to music together in the evenings when he was home. He wasn't just a hunter—he made his own bullets, an exacting and exciting hobby of molten lead and a delicate balance scale. He sewed up our Thanksgiving turkey with one hand and made new shoes for my Red Skelton doll. My father respected all those little girl things about me, but he didn't treat me like a child. One Sunday afternoon he had forty-five minutes to teach me to ride a bike and I was flying down Dore Lane with five minutes to go. Later he taught me to drive his Oldsmobile 98, a small atoll of a vehicle, in the April mud up Miller Creek, saying one lesson in turning, stopping, accelerating and backing up in that mess was all I'd need.

As I write this, he's nearly ninety-one and blind from macular degeneration. Nonetheless, we spend the first day of our 2011 Christmas vacation together comparing the birth narratives in the Gospels, figuring out that stigmata is a bunch of hooey because Jesus could not have been nailed through the palms of his hands, and reading up on the census that occasioned Mary and Joseph's return to Bethlehem. (There wasn't one.)

I still adore him.

As a kid, I also adored my brothers, who are seven and nine years older than I. They didn't have any of Daddy's powers to make things but they both had a glorious balls-to-the-wind aura that terrified and mesmerized me in equal parts. I would do anything to remind them I was alive and I made a fine target for the missile launcher on Dick's Lionel train and gave away all my allowance to Jim for the firecrackers that scared me. Sometimes the three of us or the two of them were an unbreachable whole—my aunt Mildred considered us juvenile delinquents when she tried to take care of us while Mother was in the hospital—but mostly we went our own ways.

It's easy to apply that last memory, of our separateness, to my childhood, but this winter I made my father have our old 8mm movies transferred to DVD. One of the things that struck me was how patient and kind Dick and Jim were in the Christmas scenes, opening one gift at a time for my father to film, with no tears or pouting or ripping, helping me to extract the big Chatty Cathy box from my mother's hospital corners and hangman's knots of wrapping paper and curled ribbons. They showed me how the doll worked, placed her in my arms, and turned me to the camera where I squinted at the light bar that topped the camera like a moose's antlers.

Because we were all three adopted, I worked out plans to marry one of them. I wanted to marry Dick until I was twelve years old, the day he came home from Vietnam. Jim picked him up from the airport and I came flying down the street from the school bus to see him after nearly a year of not hearing from him and he greeted me by saying, "Hi, Fatty!"

There is much to say about my brothers, who were passionate, bursting with energy and testosterone, rebellious and independent. They also possessed sweetness and protectiveness, which made me love them, and all that crackling aloofness that made me wonder about and idolize them.

•   •   •

Shakespeare would agree, I think, that first love is the most important love, with the caveat that appearances can and often do mask who or what that first love really is, and that love is as likely to lead to ruin as to paradise.

By the time I met Will, I was doomed to unrequited love.

He was in Sister Mary Martin Joseph's first grade class and

I was in Sister Mary Marcillia's. It was 1963, and each first grade classroom had fifty kids. I don't know how I found Will among the hundred kids on the first grade playground, but we both remember that each day I offered him a drink of water and proceeded to shove his face into the fountain. That was the last time I had the upper hand with Will.

Will would beg to differ.

The way he tells it, I bullied him in a Lucy-and-Charlie-Brown sort of way through second and third grade, in which we were in the same classes.

In second grade, my father gave me a big picture book called *Daddy Is a Doctor* for Christmas. I already loved to read but he! taught! me! to! read! exclamation! points! I'd never gotten a Christmas gift from my father before. I was so proud of the book and my new talent! for! reading! out! loud! that I took the book with me to school. Sister Mary Adeline read the book to the class and then went on to remark that "Daddies don't have to be doctors to be wonderful."

I was crushed. Sure, I was proud of Daddy being a doctor, but it was the fact that the book was a gift, and one he spent time enjoying with me, that made it as precious as the stone tablets with the Ten Commandments and the Magna Carta all rolled up into one. Sister's indifference was an insult to my badge of love.

Will remembers the day perfectly because he decided, after Sister read the book to the class and I ended up bawling in the hallway, that he'd show me a thing or two. Maybe his daddy worked at the paper mill, but Will swore that he would become a doctor. (In fact, he became a doctor *and* a doctorate.)

But that noon, he came over to the swings where I was waiting in line and said, "You think your dad's so great, don't you?"

"I—I—" I stuttered, wanting to explain, wanting not to cry anymore.

"I just want you to know that he went hunting with my dad." He spun on his heel and stalked away.

I brooded over his reaction the rest of the afternoon and into the evening when my father came home.

"I like Will's father," Dad said when I told him what Will said. "He's a good guy."

"I think Will was saying his daddy is as good as yours," my mother said.

Their answers weren't satisfying. That was what Sr. M. Adeline had already said. Will was saying something else, something more. Something about who and what our fathers were and what they did together. Something about their being friends. I was confused and made unhappy by my confusion. What was he trying to tell me?

Will's notice of what my father did for a living, I learn forty-five years later, turned to fantasies of adoption when my mother brought me to a birthday party. "She was elegant and kind of . . . rich, you know?" he says when I ask him about his memories of my parents.

She had beautiful legs and wore her hair in a low bun. Mother rarely got angry; the rest of the time she was smiling, her eyes brown and warm, her lipstick always fresh. I can imagine her walking me up to the front door of Mary Rose or Mary Jane or Mary Susan's house to say hello to her mother, and I can imagine how the other kids would take notice of this stylish woman and her tall, chubby, rat-haired daughter who talked and laughed too loud and walked in a second-grade-fashionable shuffle.

"She was elegant," I agree. "I never thought of her as personifying rich. She was just my mother."

"She knew everyone's name. She arched her feet. Don't you remember how she arched her feet?" he asks, and I do: watching her accelerate when driving, her foot curving out of her high heels as she pressed down on the pedal.

Our third grade memories are of the terrible experience of learning cursive writing under the tutelage of Sister Mary Francesca, aka Franny-Franny-Machine-Gun-Granny. All those hilarious stories of mean nuns you've ever heard? She was the Stalin of mean nuns.

At St. Anthony's, cursive writing was not learned in pencil. It was learned in ink—in fountain pen. There were two kinds of fountain pens: one with cartridges and one that siphoned ink out of a bottle.

I had to have the latter. It was so much easier to tattoo Will's neck with that dripping nib.* He tells me I was fond of drawing

---

* Until my inability to execute a decent Palmer Method capital "N" made Sr. M. Francesca so furious that she threw my bottle of ink at the wall, where it splattered like the blood of King Harod's martyred innocents, then made me clean it up. My mother then switched me over to a cartridge pen, sighing at one more minor incident in the parade of persecutions against her nine-year-old passing through Francesca's clutches.

fishes on him, which infuriated his mother to new heights of scolding and scrubbing. "You let that girl do anything to you!" he tells me she screamed. "Stand up for yourself!!"

Knowing Will, he remained silent as she scrubbed harder, the ink already removed. His silence would prod her to yell more as she began to scrub away skin.

"I don't care if she's bigger than you and a girl," I hear her saying as tears began rolling down his face from his burning neck. "Make her stop."

And I can hear him finally busting out: "I don't want to. I *like* her! I wish I were a Kuffel!"

"I can't believe you were dumb enough to tell your mother that," I tell him. I am sitting on a low railing in a Brooklyn Heights twilight, on my way to walk a dog. He's at home for once, taking a rare night off from the veterinary lab. His workaholism can't be a surprise to anyone reading this.

"I can't either. You know what she was like."

And I do. While I didn't know his raw neck was my fault, I was there the day after she gave him a haircut and got so carried away she stabbed him repeatedly with the scissors. "You came to school the next day with cuts along your scalp. I asked you what happened and you said you fell down. I may only have been eight years old but I knew you were lying. Why did she hate you so much?"

"I dunno. She was really smart but really poor and from a tiny town on the Montana Hi-Line. I think she wanted to go to college, maybe. She certainly didn't want to have six kids and depend on venison and wild asparagus to feed them. And

I was different from the rest, I suppose. I never felt like part of the family.

"But that really did happen, that thing with the scissors?" he asks. "You know, I have this weird thing. I don't hold grudges. You tell me a story like that and I think, 'Bless her heart.'"

"Not me," I say stridently. "And not my mother. She was crushed every time your mom threw you out of the house and you went to stay with one of your father's coworkers. She wanted you at our house."

"I wanted to be there too but my mom hated your mother so much, I was afraid she'd torch your house."

"She should have just hated me. I was the reason you had ink stains on your shirt."

"You got to start using a fountain pen first and you never let me live it down," he complains. "And remember how you used to stab me in the ear?"

"Well, excuse *me*, but my daddy *was* a doctor. I was doing you a *favor*. I didn't just stab you, I licked my red pencil and *then* I stabbed you. You coulda gotten days outta school with ear canals that red. There was method to my madness."

Another afternoon it occurs to me that the nuns might have broken us up from fourth through seventh grades on purpose.

"It didn't work," Will texts back. We were still in the same reading and math classes and somewhere in the middle grades we took to staring at each other. Will has a wide, mobile mouth, basset hound eyes the color of tallow topaz, and eyebrows that had the same coach as Nadia Comăneci. We spoke by raising one eyebrow or the other, flaring our nostrils, wiggling one ear at a time, suppressing the snorts of laughter that would have gotten us detention. Vivien Leigh's Scarlett had nothing on what we practiced while diagramming sentences.

This mutual fascination with facial tics coincided with class-wide hysteria over Helen Keller. We studied the back of the Scholastic paperback, learning the alphabet for the deaf and blind. Soon Will's long nimble fingers were flashing swear words at me whenever a teacher wasn't looking. I insulted him back and at noon he corrected my spelling.

"There's no such thing as hock spit, Francie. It h-a-w-k. I smell like hawk spit."

"No, you don't. You smell like hawk *pee*."

"Yeah?" His eyebrows shot up in a nearly perfect V and his hand danced in the air.

"That's stupid," I said. "You've never even smelled vulture shit."

At the word "shit," Lorrie McCarthy and Janet Silva stopped in their perambulation around the playground. Every day one was Micky Dolenz and the other was Davy Jones. I never understood the game because they claimed a name and then walked around talking about ordinary things like slumber parties or making gifts from macaroni.

"You could get in trouble for saying That Word," one of them advised me.

"Which word?" Will asked. "Shit or pee? I didn't *say* either of those words." His hand shot out again in a flurry. "Francie said them."

Lorrie and Janet were good girls. They remembered to turn

in their collection envelopes on Sunday and played healthfully outside after doing their homework and before setting the dinner table. When the monsignor asked the congregation to stand, raise their right hands and repeat the Legion of Decency pledge, their fathers didn't look at them sideways so as to let them know they thought the words were hooey.

More often than not, Will was either practicing the piano or had been sent to his room between coming home from school and dinner, and I was much too involved in reenacting *The Sound of Music* or reading *Jane Eyre* and eating the four cartons of Girl Scout cookies I was supposed to sell.

Put us together and Will and I trapped misbehavior like a Swiffer clings to dust, although Will never got in trouble in school. I always did, usually after following his lead. I blamed it on being such a big target, but I don't think my helpless idiot sniggering helped either. No one ever said it was bad to steep our upper lips in chocolate milk for the sake of pronounced mustaches. When he convinced me to prick my finger to look at my blood under a microscope it was in the interest of science.

We took organ lessons from Sister Mary Fina. This was essential because we practiced at noon and so got out of mandatory intramural sports. Somewhere in sixth grade, Sr. M. Fina stopped giving Will piano lessons and convinced his parents to take him to a professor at the university. I can't imagine what she said to get them to agree, but it was important because it made everyone realize Will was brilliant. "Play *Liebestraum*," my father requested in his best Bette Davis slur; we wouldn't understand the joke for years, but Will played it, from memory, and then played a run into Chopin. My father's face softened and went still, jokes gone, the afternoon gone, closing his eyes in pure pleasure. I took piano lessons, too, but "The Spinning Song" did not have that effect on him.

Was he more of a Kuffel than me? My sister-in-law could talk to him forever; my dog Lavender would fling herself on her back for his belly rub; my mother gave and got the hugs her moody adolescent daughter thought were dumb. "What a special boy," she would sigh when he left. Did Will's talent and witty politeness with my mother produce the thing that I wanted to make me special, the poems and stories I wrote, with titles like "Chaos" and "Infamy," that ran the gamut of baffled to depressed to tragic, the direct descendents of our advanced reading class's library of downers like *Flowers for Algernon, Of Mice and Men, David and Lisa*?

In 1970, in Missoula, Montana, the public school kids were practicing their French kissing while the dwindling numbers of St. Anthony seventh graders were walking in alphabetical order with precisely two floor tiles between each person, girls in one line, boys in another. Under the church portico, Mary-anne Harper whispered to a bunch of us about these weird men she heard about who had been married to unsuspecting men for years. We assumed this homo-business was a crime perpetrated by bad women on the kind of unsuspecting women we, at the age of twelve, were. There were a few couples in our class but it was rhetorical: no one went on dates, St. Anthony's didn't have dances, our first girl-boy parties happened with eighth grade graduation. As seventh graders we no longer had to wear the bib of our uniform, we'd stopped playing Barbies and some of us, I learned later, had started having periods, but we were relatively free of all that romantic stuff.

Relatively.

One Friday morning, Will Ames walked up to Mr. Fitzgerald's chalkboard to work on an equation to determine the volume of a golf ball. I know that it was a Friday and I know that it was a second Friday in the month, the day we were allowed to dress out of uniform. So instead of wearing his daily black trousers, white shirt and forest green sweater, Will was wearing white bellbottoms and a red shirt with collar points nearly to his elbows. I drummed my fingers on my notebook and thought, "Ames has a great butt. Ames is great. I'm . . .

". . . in . . . love . . . with Will Ames."

I could never let anyone know this secret. I weighed somewhere between 190 and 240* pounds and had thick blocky hair. Sister Mary Theodore had recently taken me aside to tell me I needed to wear a slip and deodorant. My brother Dick, who would these days probably be diagnosed as having borderline personality disorder, enjoyed nothing more than jeering "Fatty" and "Faggy" at me, and I had no reason to disagree. I thought "faggot" meant being bad at sports.

In love and in despair, I walked around in a cloud of confu-

---

* I remember a diet in sixth grade, at the start of which I weighed in the 170s. It lasted about ten days. The next time I remember looking at a scale, I was fifteen and weighed 240 pounds. I found the scale useful only when I went on diets.

sion. Will and I weren't a couple, but we hung out more than the few announced couples, who might only sit together on the bus or talk on the phone. I'd watched my brothers date, go to the prom and marry too young, but all of that was beyond my life of babysitting for fifty cents an hour and getting around on a one-speed Schwinn. On the day before that second Friday, Will made me laugh from my belly. By the time we were in the choir loft at noon, I was laughing from my heart and my throat, breathlessly, as he played and sang his perverse, rolling-R lyrics to the tune of "Those Were the Days":

> *We dined on garbage,*
> *On rot-ton garbage*
> *We'd sing and dine forever and a day . . .*

My giggles pleased him. That was the first thing I figured out.

Mocking love was the second thing I figured out. The nuns put us in the same eighth grade class where twenty-four times a million raging hormones harassed a young teacher, Mrs. Donaldson. Will and I were caught passing notes under our desktops and she moved us across the room from each other. Our old staring game turned into a rubber-lipped imitation of some characters we had seen Carol Burnett and Harvey Korman perform, in which we twitched and quivered eyebrows and noses in imitation of extreme horniness, pulling our lips between our teeth. Our performance of desire was like watching a five-year-old dance *Giselle*: it may have been technically proficient but there was no sexual fire behind it.

I was romantic but not sexual in grade school.* The pages in which Rochester tortures Jane Eyre with the threat of sending her away, only to propose marriage, were thick with a wide variety of cookie crumbs, as was Mr. Darcy's explanatory letter to Lizzie.† But I didn't daydream about kissing or touching.

This was not true for Will. We were pretty sure that unmarried sex was a sin, and nobody ever mentioned sex that was not sex, such as boys masturbating together. But Will had several complicated secretive relationships with male classmates. This group of boys behaved, I learned later, a lot like you'd expect young girls and boys would. Boys got dropped and picked up by other boys and jealousies were rife. The code of silence was absolute. If Will didn't tell me, then certainly no other boy told his busmate girlfriend. I think the straight boys thought of it as they did basketball and choosing teams and envying someone else's talent. For Will, however, it was his first experience of the overtly erotic. It was, for him, a beginning that had to last another four years until he went to college.

To protect my dignity but keep Will close to my heart, I considered how to cinch best friendship with an iron grip. I was his greatest fan and his closest confidante and I made sure he got as many invitations to dinner at my house as possible. I

---

* That ended the summer between eighth grade and high school, when I read *The Godfather*.

† And consider how enticing it was to me that Rochester overlooked Jane Eyre's plainness or that Darcy fell in love despite himself.

had numerous friends at St. Anthony's, but I began to withdraw a bit, focusing on Will and on whatever it took to keep him attached at my hip. We played endless board games in our basement, I read the same books he chose from our reading group library. I did this in a way that didn't smother him—the way Katie Keanon did. She was a small, odd person who also fell head over heels for Will and showed it by sending him flowers and chocolates and love letters. It embarrassed him and I played her for all she was worth before hauling off and lobbing a chalk-filled eraser at the back of his green sweater. Maybe Katie Keanon was ready to look doe-eyedly stupid in front of everybody, but I wouldn't be caught dead revealing how I felt.

*   *   *

It was the infancy of the '70s, the Age of Aquarius, an era of pop loyalty that promised we could be there for each other with songs like "You've Got a Friend," "Bridge Over Troubled Water," "I Don't Know How to Love Him," and "With a Little Help from My Friends."

*   *   *

It's a Saturday night when I call Will not just to reminisce but to ask, after all these years, who we were and what happened to us. "Why did you like me?" I ask him as I settle into my pillows and my dog settles against me. After forty-nine years I'm not particularly surprised that he is as askance that I liked him as I am for being liked.

"Well, you. Then your mom." Will is a scientist, a well-known endocrinology researcher. He takes his time in responding to the question, careful to answer in an organized and factored way. "Then your house.* The ditch.† Your father was always home, reading, and I was terrified by him but I also felt accepted by him, almost appreciated. You know, as a misfit. Like he thought, *That Willy is the perfect companion for Francie.*"

"Were you ever in love with me?" I ask. This question is a huge risk. I gave him seven years of my young life and this might be the first time I've broached the subject with him. "You know," I hurry on, "in that crushy way."

Tomorrow Will turns fifty-five years old. I want to celebrate his once having had a crush on me.

"Oh, no-o-o," he says. "You were much too important to me to have a crush on."

Good answer, Will.

---

* We had a large house that should have been designated by the National Trust for Historic Preservation because it was such an exquisite example of the early sixties ranch style. If anything could be "built in"—a blender, a rotisserie, a television—it was. Plus it had a shrine to the Virgin Mary and was almost entirely paneled in teak.

† An irrigation ditch system, lined by old willows, bordered our yard, which was surrounded on two sides by massive fields. The ditch bifected in one of those fields and had wooden floors and trusses. It was a magnificent ditch.

"Did I ever hurt you?" he asks. My eyebrows shoot up. I'm the one trying to reconstruct the best and most ruinous relationship of my life, the one that helped set me up for the purgatory of not just spinsterhood but deep longing for a friend.

"Uh, yeah," I say, like, duh, Bullwinkle.

"Really?" he asks sharply and curiously.

Actually he administered three deathblows to my heart, but I tell him about the one that exemplified best how he could plunge me into mourning.

First, though, you have to know that when Will and I went to public high school, drift was inevitable and, on his part, desirable. Although we'd had different homerooms from fourth through seventh grades, we were in the same by-subject classes, cheek-by-jowl through the Goths and Vandals, predicate nouns and Confirmation instruction. In high school, our schedules were different. Electives separated us further. He was making friends in his choices of Spanish and chemistry, and I was failing Russian Novels and German. We were both thespians— along with Kevin, who Will remembers fondly*—but Will was by far the more successful of us. He was funny, evil, musical. I was so serious about acting that I could only do tragedy. Will got leads and won prizes. I did not. He was in choir and the select singing groups and edited the newspaper.† He got As, and

---

* "You could balance champagne glasses on his butt."

† Which I got kicked off of. His fame for writing also put a serious crimp in what had been my territory of specialness.

his cadre of tiny, petite girls with long blonde hair and great tits depleted whatever hope I was managing to hang on to in those awful years. Their physical attributes were beyond what any diet could ever endow me with. Among all of his minions, it was Kat who became his New Best Friend.

I made five-minute friends and was unsatisfied because they weren't Will, couldn't make me laugh or think or try the way he did. Had our yearbook had captions under our graduation pictures, mine would have been "Most Depressed and Best Underachiever."

Still, Will didn't quite let go. He might show up with Kat to give her a tour of my house or we'd go to the occasional movie together. Kat and I became uneasy friends. She was the first woman I could really talk to about books and writing and music, but she was tiny and sexually precocious and I felt like a bumbling Macy's parade cartoon next to her. We are still uneasy friends, spending at least as much time not speaking to each other as being the best of pals.

One of those times Will sought me out was an evening in our last year of high school. We headed to the basement, as we always did. My father had installed an old slot machine and a professional-quality pool table that we mostly used to zoom the balls around without bothering with cues or any desire to sink them. The pool balls were like worry beads, and I was worrying mightily as Will sat and slowly pedaled on the stationary bike and explained a few things.

"I'm gay, France."

Silence except for the soft banking of a pool ball.

"I like guys."

"But you hang out with girls."

"But I don't want to fuck them."

"You're always talking about how beautiful and sexy Kat is."

"That's because she is. She's the most beautiful girl I know."

"Does *she* know you're gay?"

"Of course."

I could taste the bile on the back of my tongue.

"Why would you want to fuck a guy?" I tried to imagine what this entailed. The only thing I could conjure up was two men rubbing the tips of their penises together in imitation of the missionary position, which was the only sexual configuration I'd figured out. *The Godfather* didn't have any queer killers and I was too heavy to absorb the scenes of Sonny Corleone fucking a woman against a wall.

"I don't know. I just do."

"Who do you want to fuck?"

"No one."*

"I don't get it," I said. "I think it's weird."

"We're thespians, France. Who do you think likes to act? You've known other guys who've come out. It's not like I'm the first."

"Yeah, but you're *you*." The boy I, by then, dreamed about

---

* Now, of course, I know that's a lie. He had a crush on Mark Fallon. Where there's a crush there's . . . Still, what else could he say to me at the time? It was dangerous knowledge.

the missionary position with, about touching me. The boy I looked at and really did quiver as my nipples hardened.

On his way out, he hugged my mother good-bye with tears in his eyes. "I love you, Will," she said, and he swiped his arm across his face. "Thank you, Mrs. Kuffel. I love you, too."

One more betrayal, I thought. My mother was wondering if he would take me to the prom—and he was gay. On top of that, I hadn't known it in the twelve years since I pushed his head into the drinking fountain. A pile of betrayal.

And then in the summer between our freshman and sophomore years in college, Will, Kat, and Lawrence, another friend from high school, all worked at Mario's, where Missoula ate its first manicotti. Will was studying piano in Arizona. Kat was a precocious poet at the University of Montana, and Lawrence was going to college in Chicago.

Had anyone asked, I would have said I was the same Francie Kuffel all of them had known for years. Sad, ponderous, alienated. I had made one change, though. That summer I took a course from a professor whom our high school honors English teacher had spoken of as the most brilliant teacher of Shakespeare who never gave As. I'd tucked that sentence away as a silent challenge and got an A in the junior-level study of tragedies.

That A was my talisman against the bullshit of high school and the accomplishments and independence of my friends. They would have been impressed by that A for approximately one second before turning the conversation back to whoever they were having—or wanted to have—sex with and whatever other topics thin kids talked about. But I had begun to strike back.

One night, out of the blue, Mary called. Mary was a year younger than Kat, Will and I, and had spent her senior year as an exchange student in Japan. She wanted to reconnect with old friends. "Would you give me a ride over to Mario's?" she asked.

My heart sank so quickly that she could have heard it over the phone if she'd known what the noise was. It was one of those moments when you know you're agreeing to a bad idea. I had seen very little of Will and Kat that summer. He was working a couple of jobs to supplement his music scholarship in Arizona and she was living with a guy in the MFA program. I was in summer school and therapy, where we talked a lot about Will and Kat and agreed it was best not to see them much. When I did, on occasion, join them for a gin and tonic at the dark red-lit gay bar called the Flame, they were full of plans to move to New York City as soon as possible, talking about Keith Jarrett and Robert Altman and Bartók, smug with the esoteric pleasures of Kat's graduate school friends and their parties. Behind, it seemed, in everything except *Hamlet*, I could keep up only with what could be bought or explained, as Will did when he played me the *Concerto for Orchestra* and pointed out the section in the intermezzo in which the violins take up the melody only to be laughed down, honkingly, by the horns. "That's you, France." I looked at him and didn't dare ask if I was the violins or the snickering brass.

Unable to say no to Mary, I drove over and picked her up. She was excited to see everyone and I hung back, near the door, silent and lumbering and ashamed. Lawrence called me the next day and admitted that after we left, Will turned to Kat and said, "That was Francie trying to prove she has other friends," at which Kat smirked and probably went back to jiggling her boobs for extra tips.

Never has anyone fallen out of love faster. It was the last truth that broke the camel's back. Like the Bartók horns, he truly disdained me. There was so much of Will I wanted, vampire-like, to absorb and be. He held the future in his skills and lack of family connection. The little I had was the past or pointless—that A in Shakespeare, my bedroom that looked out over the old willow trees swaying like the Oregon ocean, my therapist, my family's house on Flathead Lake. They were small, now, offering very little toward adulthood. He was excited to grow up and I was afraid. He had left me behind long ago and I didn't know it had happened until that night when he held up a mirror to me and I saw nothing but the restaurant door in its reflection.

I didn't speak to Will for the next ten years. I didn't need to. His words were the judge's gavel. His words followed me back to school. I failed a poetry workshop that fall because I was so frozen I couldn't withdraw, and too frozen by Kat's presence in it to attend. I went to school in London the following winter and there began to put the ghosts behind me. I watched Vladimir Ashkenazy's hands blur through a performance and could see that there was more to Bartók than the *Concerto for Orchestra*, more to the piano than Will. I made friends with the students in my study program and traveled and went to the ballet with them. When I returned to Missoula, Kat and Will had moved to New York. A little battered, friendless after being abroad for a year, I could make *my* start on life.*

.   .   .

Will is appalled at the story. He has a lovely quality of forgiving and forgetting. I laugh and say, "I'm al-l-l about revenge. I never forget and I rarely forgive." He is silent in a way that asks what I'm planning to do to punish him for that night thirty-five years ago when he confirmed everything I feared most about myself. I laugh. "Don't worry, honey. You fall into the category of rare forgiveness. And anyway, I came to understand a long time ago that when we were kids I wanted to be you and you wanted to be me and neither of us could forgive each other for that."

"Mmm. Maybe. I definitely wanted to be a Kuffel but you were part of the package. It wouldn't have been any *fun* without you."

At which I begin to cry.

---

* Which truly began when Grace Willoughby, Kevin's little sister, who I had a vague recollection of being in the Joni Mitchell set in high school, walked up to me outside a philosophy class and said, "You're Frances Kuffel, aren't you? You look interesting. Do you want to have coffee?"

• • •

Unwittingly, Will and I settled on a ten-year plan in which once a decade we would try to be friends. It took a couple of trial runs to get it right. Therapy helped. Achievement helped. He became a doctor, I became a literary agent; his research led to a vast amount of publication and international seminars, I began to write in earnest. When I published my first book, before Will and I reestablished contact, I thought to myself, *Well, Ames, we're even. You've spent your life working on diabetes and I'm touching a lot of lives that are prone to it.*

Not surprisingly, the confidence of *Passing for Thin* prodded me to find his email address and wish him a happy birthday after not speaking for twenty-nine years.

"There isn't a day that goes by that I don't hear your voice," he wrote back. "I'll hear you on my deathbed."

• • •

Will Ames was the first boy and the first man I was in love with. It lasted eight years and is in many ways the template for all of the other important crushes and love affairs I've had. It wasn't until my mid-forties, when I was in a normal-sized body, that admitting to having feelings for a man didn't take months of therapy and, usually, having to get drunk. That was also when I began to date and, for a few months at a time, have boyfriends. In the five years of knowing Dar I had gained a lot of weight back but had not lost all of my hard-found ability to openly want to be with a man. I didn't learn that skill from Will, but the outcome of it has been weirdly similar. Men love to talk to me. Sometimes they fall in love with me. They always fall out of love with me and then dance fast and long to keep me as a friend.

Dar had gone from the amazed first conversations to dancing. He'd simply skipped the middle part.

*   *   *

In two things, I am very lucky.

I am tenacious. I can struggle inwardly with my feelings and wait forever for the object of them to come to his senses and realize he has them, too. When he doesn't—and in my experience, no one ever has—I've perfected the waiting game well enough to survive the inevitable bomb of the truth.

And I never forget. Will and I picked up at exactly the moment before things went wildly out of balance. My brother comments that he always knows when I've talked to Will because for the next several hours, my eyes dance, I am animated and kind of silly, my ghosts of loneliness and fear drop away. Will is my human equivalent to an antianxiety drug. As is Kevin, whom I depend on as I try to figure out where it all went wrong with Dar.

"It's because I've gained so much weight," I say.

"I thought you looked great," Kevin says. "You couldn't have gained ugliness in the weeks between Seattle and Santa Fe."

"It's because I'm stupid about music."

"No. You're stupid about the music he knows about and you don't."

"If I spoke Spanish and knew how to scuba dive—"

"—or you sprouted wings and could fly. How 'bout that, Tinker Bell?"

"Tinker Bell was pretty uptight, too," I remind him. "Dar thinks I'm tense."

"Try *in*tense. You don't let people off the hook very easily."

"I'm sorry." I backtrack immediately. "How have I hooked you?"

"I dunno but you have. I've never told anyone the things I've told you. I think it's because nothing shocks you. I trust you because of that. No one takes pictures of me, and you were snapping away down on the piers and I was mugging like America's Next Top Model. You just *do* that."

"It's because I love you," I say. "I talked to you and fell in love and then I saw you and I fell more in love. You can't do anything to make me change that. Even taking a bad picture doesn't make me not love you." I laugh. I can understand why Kevin Willoughby, the Cutest Boy in High School, is sensitive about having a camera aimed at him.

"It's because you love me more than your baggage"—a standing joke he has. "It's because you love *my* baggage."

"I loved Dar when his baggage was all over my floor," I wail.

"That wasn't his baggage, honey. That was his bags. He was high on crack but the real question is *why* was he high on crack?"

I can only think of generalities. He was, I tell Will, who actually met him, unsatisfied with his life. He had been deeply satisfied teaching grade schoolers and building houses in Nicaragua. Coming back to work in IT in New York must have felt empty and pointless. He hadn't felt that way when he and his wife moved to New York after school, but signing on with that nonprofit had redefined him.

"Uh, France?" Will says when I end my rant. "Have you thought about the word 'wife'?"

Will and Kevin, being gay, don't date in a world where everyone our age has been divorced. They've had serious relationships that involved custody of dogs and KitchenAid mixers when they ended, but I've almost stopped thinking about past marriages. Divorce is like bronchitis: At some point everybody's had it.

Except me, of course. I spent the better part of fifty years hiding behind being guys' best pal, having no faith they could love me. So what do I know, really?

"Who divorced whom?" Will asks.

"She did."

"Was it bitter?"

"I don't know. Dar kinda makes it sound like a childish mistake."

"He's only forty, France. If he was divorced for a couple of years before he met you, they *were* children."

"They were college sweethearts," I tell him.

"Don't you think you'd better move on?" he asks.

I sigh. "Kevin says the same thing. 'You don't have to sit around like you weigh 300 pounds anymore,'" I mimic. "Except I more or less do."

"I've always thought you were pretty."

"Right," I snort. "That's why you ignored me for Kat and all the cool girls."

"I didn't say I thought you had great tits, France. I said I think you're pretty. And a lot more. You don't have to sit around being all depressed about Dar. Go get over him."

"What's the point? I'm fifty-three."

"Fifty-three is the new thirty-three."

"Yeah, you can say that. You're still fifty-two."

He chuckles his evil, smug chuckle, but the days are getting longer—June and fifty-three are coming his way.

"I'm tired of men," I whine. "I have Daisy. I want to move to Seattle. I want to write a novel."

"So write about dating," Dr. Will says. "You write about everything else you do."

*   *   *

I call Kevin a few hours later. "Who was the first guy you were really, really in love with?"

"Greg Alexander," he answers promptly. They were in the same class in high school, were in choir together and hung out for a while in the same gonzo group of snow-heads and guests at a rich friend's Georgetown Lake cabin where there was plenty of pot, beer and acid. Greg cleaned up when he decided to take over Sentinel High School government, and he and Kevin saw less of each other after that, and although they have spoken about the big events in their adult lives, Kevin has never told

Greg how he felt. "In fact," he adds, "I've never told anyone about Greg, but oh my God, I think about him every day."

I hang up and call Will again. He acts all put out at my pestering, but his answer is almost the same. Brian Schwarz was a cutie-pie nonentity in the class of '75, but Will squeals when he talks about him. "The. Cutest. Boy. Who. Ever. Lived."

So it turns out that, in a way, my two best friends, one of whom I wanted to have children with, have the same template as I. We were silently, hopelessly, distantly in love with a boy in high school and learned to date later (much later, in my case). Dar is someone who knows how to walk up to a girl he sees around campus and marry her.

I email my agent the next day to tell her the Santa Fe trip was a disaster and I want to write about looking for love and coffee among the wreckage of late middle age.

And then I click on craigslist.

Three

A snail's reproductive organs are in its head.

"I am bored," I posted. I was hoping some polycentric or film studies professor would catch my reference to George Sanders's suicide note. I added a photo and confirmed my ad.

Two hours later I had forty-four responses. Like I said, craigslist never disappoints. It had not only brought Dar but two other sporadic love affairs and one epic phone sex boyfriend, one of the few men who's walked me up to and through an orgasm.

Unlike the so-called real dating websites, craigslist's losers are up front and hold no promise of a caffeine buzz. There were dozen of boys requesting fellatio,* offerings of massage† and stating interest.‡

* "Did you read the part about being bored?" I responded.

† Followed, I assumed, by fellatio.

‡ "I'm interested" is *not* the correct answer to "I'm bored." I mean, if my boredom is interesting it must not be boredom, right?

It was, however, an opportunity to expand my repertoire. I could now, by tapping a few keys in reply to this message, be a cougar *and* have a butler: "I'm a handsome, 21-year-old guy who works out. Do you need things done around your apt, home or office? I do those chores! I will accompany you shopping, drive you to an appointment? Draw you a bath? A date for brunch, lunch, dinner, weddings, any events, parties, movies, coffee, drinks, any type of night out . . . or laid back evenings in! Anytime of DAY!! . . . AVAILABLE MORNINGS AND AFTERNOONS!! Get what you want . . . the first time!"*

I don't "do" peppy. I was exhausted just from reading his email.

. . .

I may go out with men, but I date my friends.

I forwarded the following conundrum to Will in a storm of glee. His boyfriend, Rico, is an over-the-top romantic and I was sure he'd have a reaction. " 'I am a caucasian [sic] thus a very touchy feely and romantic man which some women may not want.' Since when are Caucasians noted for their affectionate behavior?" I asked.

---

* Yes, this is a word-for-word quote. He did not write under his real name and I never responded, so I knew nothing more about him than his misuse of question marks.

"If he were French or Italian, he'd say so," he said. "He might be South American."

"Or he's from those mountains, the whatcha-call-ems—?"

"The Caucasus? Maybe it's so cold there you have to snuggle in order to survive."

My friend Bette was more direct. "Allow me to translate. 'I am caucasian' = 'I'm a white guy with little education and I don't wanna date no smart black women.' 'Very touchy feely' = 'I'm a groper and I treat nipples like radio knobs.' 'Romantic man which some women may not like' means 'I hide the fact that I'm a misogynist by buying flowers—cheap ones—controlling where and when we eat dinner—which means cheap—and I drive a late-model truck that I drive as if it were a penis.'"

I relayed all of this to Kevin. I knew he was shaking his head as he wrote back. "Don't let this get around, Frances, but I'm about to break the Code of Silence from the Captain Midnight Society. He is an insecure white dude who cries when he doesn't get his way and threatens suicide when you break up with him. And by the way? I drive my truck like a penis. Some things are male even if you have chintz curtains."

•   •   •

At least the Caucasian cuddler was, well, taking note of the craigslist heading "Woman Looking for Man."

"What's the most expensive pair of shoes you have and what color is your favorite in shoes?" another man wrote. "Do you wear heels?"

For a giggle, I replied with a picture of my most gorgeous Cydwoqs, which could be described as Dolly Parton cowboy boots meet one of the elven princesses from *Lord of the Rings*. His response was a chagrined admission of a fetish. Would that scare me away?

I yawned. Amid so many photos of willies green from camera flashes in bathrooms, a guy into Jimmy Choos was a Dobie Gillis of normality.

Who knew how fascinated men could be with women's fashion? I certainly hadn't imagined we'd be *comparing* clothes until I read, "I would like to meet for a fun nite [sic] of me getting all dressed up for you, nothing else. I am a regular guy [and I] have all my own clothes, make-up, etc. [I] do have a picture."*

As I continued deleting, I amassed some maybe-obvious rules of courtship that, abetted by the decoder ring a couple of Ovaltine proof-of-purchase seals will get you, should save time.

- ***Delete*** *all emails accompanied by photos of a man's weenie—especially if he has taken it himself, and especially if he took it in the bathroom mirror.*

- ***Delete*** *all emails cribbed from bad pop songs ("hi really I wanna know you").*

- ***Delete*** *all emails written in textese ("why u so board [sic]? do u want 2 talk on the phone?").*

---

* But a picture of which you?

These deletions are called for because they break the first Rule of Courtship:

- ***If a guy is too lazy to spell or punctuate, your relationship is already over.***

I kept digging. Finally, a responder named Sol asked what kind of man would dispel my boredom. I took Daisy for a walk while I thought about that and ended up writing back, "Someone literate, with an imagination who follows through; someone who will be patient in coaxing me out of a self-imposed isolation I'm finding hard to break. Someone amusing."

That was a fair answer except for the line about following through, which means, from too much experience on my part, that phone sex* is all very well, but living it is better than imagining it.

"Let's meet for coffee on Saturday at 4," Sol wrote back. "Meet me in Bleecker Street Park."

One of my perversions is that whenever someone sets up a date with me, I automatically want to cancel or change it.

---

* A note on phone sex: For someone who is inexperienced and/or insecure, phone sex is a good tool for breaking through all those words, acts, costumes and casts of characters that our mothers and churches would be appalled to know we harbor.

Well, most churches. I'm a malpracticing Catholic. My church may be a pioneer in these matters.

"I don't feel like going into the city," I told my therapist, Dr. A-Cigar-Is-Not-a-Cigar.

"Just do it," he advised. "You need to get out and meet new people."

"Can we make it five?" I emailed Sol.

"No," he wrote back.

So I put on four o'clock coffee date clothes, reassured Daisy I'd be home soon and set off for the Village.

It had been years since I'd been this far west of Seventh Avenue, or maybe it was the glittering May light and almost-summer heat that made the walk from Christopher Street, through a street fair among the fashionable shoppers, kaleidoscopic. I began to get excited for a walk-and-talk with window shopping and making up stories about people. I hoped Sol would have sized up this gem of a day exactly as I had. I sat on a bench and looked at my watch. I had ten minutes before I could expect him to show up, so I turned my attention to a Big Red Bus disgorging a load of women who giggled their way over to Magnolia Bakery. They wore fragile shoes and screeched that they were *already full* after one bite of dessert and that they should *get a picture of* all *of us eating our cupcakes.*

On the edges of the gaggles of girls with their cupcakes were the chubby girls, dressed in clothes too tight, trying too hard to twist themselves into the Good Girlfriend image of Charlotte or Miranda.

Ah, my sisters, the wannabes. I know you well, although it

is part of Einstein's Theory of Relativity that no two wannabes can inhabit the same space. Age and distance give me compassion. I've been a wannabe longer than you've been alive. In the deep shade of the brick and iron park, I watch how the Carries desperately need their plump pals in order to make their fantasy—and their prettiness—come alive. If only the plumpies knew they complete the story. If only the plumpies would simply take their cupcakes and *go*. The Carries would melt like frosting on a manhole cover.

*   *   *

I was feeling more *Annie Hall* than *Sex in the City*. This Sol-guy, now five minutes late, had sounded smart and I was feeling decidedly that the day was rare and should not be wasted in Starbucks.

After ten minutes I strolled around, looking for a solo guy also scanning the crowd. I recircled the park and noticed a thin man with a straggly gray braid reading on a bench. He looked up and said, "Fran—" as I said, "Sol—"

He kissed me hello and we exchanged the patter we should have exchanged in email or on the phone. I told him I was a writer and he told me he had recently produced a movie, had published several books and had been a food writer for a magazine I didn't recognize. "I live two blocks away. Do you want to have a glass of wine in my garden?"

If we weren't going to make fun of people or finger the cheap

Indian shirts at the street fair, sitting in a West Village garden was second best.

It became third best when he put his arm around my waist and began caressing my butt.

"Is this a one-off?" I asked as we crossed Bank Street.

"I don't know."

The building shared the garden. He didn't offer to go up and get the wine but he did lean over and begin kissing me. After three minutes of being a spectacle for everyone whose windows faced east, he said, "Let's go upstairs."

How many things had happened in the last eight minutes that were telling me this was a b-a-a-d idea?

Why did I allow him to point me up the stairs, pushing me gently on my buttocks?

Dr. A-Cigar-Is-Not-a-Cigar would have said I wanted to fuck my father in the guise of this man who looked older than me and had done so much more professionally than I had. My friend Jean would have said, with regretful triumph, that I had wanted it, and her husband, Ben, would have said it was the sort of thing he used to do before Jean but that I deserved better. Bette and Will were a fifty-fifty bet on either, "Go for it!" or "Call a cab. *Now*." As for me, I was mostly feeling thirsty. A diet 7UP would have been perfect on that hot afternoon. Or maybe a Fresca.

After hitting my head on the braces of his loft bed in the ensuing gymnastics, I pushed him off and out, sat up and began looking for my clothes.

"What's the matter?" he asked. "Did you enjoy any of it?"

"You're fine," I said as I pulled on my blouse and looked around for my tank top and prepared to leave without it if necessary. "But we have stuff in common. We could go out. This is ruining it. You have my number—call me." I found my tank top and squished it into my bag.

• • •

My answering machine was flashing when I got home.

"Sorry, girl," it played back. "I guess it's just too soon after the breakup."

"Ya think he coulda maybe mentioned the breakup before now?" I asked Daisy, as she pressed her head against my hard rubbing, her plainspoken way of telling me she needs love and reassurance when I've been away. "What Burt Bacharach song d'ya think he thinks he's acting out?" Daisy licked my hand and collapsed for a quick belly rub before I went in to run a very hot bath of Crabtree & Evelyn Nantucket Briar. As the bubbles piled reassuringly up, I called Kevin.

"I walked out on a guy in the middle of sex!" I crowed. I had decided this was a victory, not going any further than I felt like.

"You what?"

"I met this guy, supposedly for coffee. He only wanted sex. In the middle of it I realized I was bored so I stopped and left."

"Uh . . . Good, I guess."

"Aren't you proud of me? Usually I go through with it because I don't want to hurt someone's feelings."

"Did you ever think about not *starting* it because it would hurt *your* feelings?"

I splashed into the suds as carefully as I could to keep the phone dry. "What does the Big Book say? 'Progress not perfection'?"

"I'm HIV positive, Frances. On this subject I've learned perfection the hard way. I'm giving Grace a pedicure, Frances. Can I call you back?" There was mumbling on his end of the connection. "Or can Grace call you back? She has a few things she wants to say to you."

Later that night, Grace and Kevin scolded me into an admission of my wrongs. Yes, it was dangerous. Yes, I was spineless to follow him up Greenwich Street. And yes, the worst of it was he had a *braid*. I promised to be wiser.

· · ·

I predicated the next date with a number of phone calls that turned into phone sex. When he came over, I got an orange rose and souvlaki in return for a jaw-numbing blowjob before the email saying, "I thought I was ready but I'm not."

I don't know when women are ready to start paddling out to sea again, but men have the special problem of *thinking* they are able to shtup a snake if it stands up long enough. Another piece of unforgivably bad male thinking is their inability to weigh the sixty-four-million-dollar question everyone is hiding from each other—baggage.

Quibble over the nuances as much as you want, but there are two kinds of romantic baggage: the kind we can abandon

LOVE SICK

and start to walk away from, and the kind we heave into the nearest therapist's office. *This is* not *rocket science, guys!* If you spend your dinner hours and weekends in existential angst, keep the woody you talked yourself into at home.

Sol and Orange Rose Guy had the most dangerous kind of baggage: self-ignorance. I was barely a month away from crying on the empty Phoenix freeways on my way home from Dar's, but at least I knew the chances of finding "another" Dar would be impossible, or a different piece to fit my puzzle would be slim. But practicality had already set in.

Tip: The best way to get over a man is to start dating another man.

Be prepared to settle, to be fond rather than ragingly in love, to share a couple of nights a week together instead of every minute, to lean on your girlfriends for fun as much as on the New Maybe—but go out and reassure yourself you're wantable. We—men and women—are always ready to be wantable.

Not being ready is a notion I defy. Ha!

If either Sol or Orange Rose Guy were truly Not Ready, they wouldn't have replied to the ad, so there are two excuses I can offer in their defense.

The most reasonable is that they thought they had kicked the habit of at least the sexual side of life with the ex but found out that sex stirs all kinds of stuff up.

The other explanation is that it was I. I am a deeply pessimistic person. My water glass isn't half empty, it's half empty and radioactive. It's easy for me to go from thinking of myself as *a* Wrong Woman to *the* Wrong Woman to just plain Wrong.

63

Dar, in rejecting me for not being into his music, rock climbing and scuba diving, could make me feel Wrong but I was fighting it, so far with guys who made me feel wiser if not smarter.

Not that it's any easier being a Right Woman when faced with a Wrong Man. I don't have a lot of experience being the dumper, but I can see that it might be a good idea to have a patter for why there won't be a second date. At least the too-soon shtick, a more substantial version of it's not you, it's me absolves everyone except the original heartbreaker.

But really? Being ready to drop my jeans before coffee makes the original heartbreaker look better than ever. She at least had the self-respect to get rid of the guy.

· · ·

One problem with dating in one's fifties is that one or both suspects are likely to harbor the grief or disbelief of a broken, long relationship, usually a marriage, usually with children.

Advancing middle age should be the first time since childhood that we can really indulge ourselves without feeling selfish. This means no unfair competition in our love lives.

Tip: Beware the ex but carry garlic if he has a daughter.

The man with a daughter over the age of about eleven is probably dating her, not you. Sons are low maintenance for dads, possibly because they can take each other's interests for granted. But the moment Daddy's Little Pumpkin develops bumps on her chest, she becomes the treasure he must protect like a Kumari princess.

"She's in sixth grade and friends with everybody," one date expounded. "She's doing soccer and plays piano and flute." He stops and smiles at his hands folded on the table between us. "For years, the only way we could get her to sleep was playing 'In-A-Gadda-Da-Vida.' All seventeen minutes. Go figure."

That paternal bafflement? A shameless lie. In college she is the delight of holidays and summers, more dateable than any other woman.

"What's she like?" I had asked Orange Rose Guy of his daughter during the stiff dinner we shared after the blow job and before the not-ready email.

"She's beautiful and talented. She interned with the Wooster Group last summer and she's interested in either going back or joining a company like Bond Street after she graduates from Sarah Lawrence."

"And your son?" He was tucking into the local diner's meat loaf as though he needed, urgently, to kill it.

"He went to art school to become a cartoonist. Still living with his mother, still . . . drawing, I guess. I need to take him out to dinner this week, see what's going on."

At some point, the daughter falls in love with someone besides Daddy. Enter the ex, who is of practical value in fashioning the princess their princess has always wanted to be, but it's Daddy who pays and whose approval adds that extra royal cachet.

"My daughter wants to show me a place in Kent Island for the wedding," Martin, another mid-fifties divorcé, said as we snuggled into our respective beds before talking dirty.

"Is that someplace amazing?" I asked. I wasn't sure what

exactly Martin did for a living, but he had some kind of security background because he told me he'd matched a recording of my voice on the phone against one of my TV interviews posted on YouTube to make sure I was who I said I was. For some reason he wanted his imaginary sex to come from a verifiable woman.

"I'm sure it is. At least it checks out okay. I'll know more after I see it."

I wondered if he meant that no known Taliban members were waiters or if the cliff it sits on isn't likely to break off in the next rain. "So. What is she wearing?"

He grunted. "This is no laughing matter and it's going to cost me an arm and a leg. She's a good kid, though. She's in law school. She's earned her reception on the Bay."

Suddenly I wasn't so much in the mood.

And trust me (because I'm one, too), Princess *enjoys* being Daddy's Number One. How do you think I learned the lyrics to "Thank Heaven for Little Girls"? I was my daddy's princess for a few sweet years of sitting on his shoulders and styling his hair. All that coziness ended when I began to gain weight and no longer sat on laps or got humped around like a sack of giggling potatoes. On the other hand, my father was my date in the dateless desert of high school. Whenever my mother was out of town, we had dinner at Bug's Barbecue and went to a movie. He introduced me to Mel Brooks ("It's twue, it's twue"), the Marx Brothers ("Booga-booga!") and Charlie Chaplin. I—and the entire audience in the tiny hippie theater—had never seen anyone laugh harder than my father through Flip the Frog shorts . . . until he began crying with laughter during Chaplin's dinner of spaghetti and streamers.

So what I missed out on by not sitting on my father's lap I gained later when he taught me "Minnie the Moocher."

Take that, Da-Vida.

*   *   *

Tip: It's no longer what you do for a living, but when you do it.

People in their fifties fall into one of three work categories: traditional worker bees, freelance, or retired.

What the swinging fifties don't want to admit, I think, is how much we value a partner who has leisure time. How tied is the fifty-five-year-old worker bee to the office? If he hates his job, he's too old to remain unsoured and unbowed by it. The full-time job is the equivalent of another ex, and how he feels about his fifty-hour week can create the resentment of a divorce. On the other hand, if he's too happy at his job, he risks being both boring and unavailable.

At this age, I'm hoping Mr. Extension 6651 can check up on his staff while taking Tuesday off for the Orchid Show.

This is why Mr. Done It is in a lot of demand. The best retiree is the man who made his tick and decided—chose, preferred, elected—to retire early enough to enjoy his [comparative] youth. Mr. Done It is a happy man, pleased with his cleverness and pleased to play in the spare time he created.

Which leaves the hipster-slacker, Mr. Freelance. (A word of caution: The description "self-employed" is very different from "freelance." Freelancers tend to have thought about and embrace the notion of being a knight errant, Sir Gawain or Walter Raleigh, riding their wits and networks rather than horses or galleons. The self-employed, on the other hand, place more emphasis on "employment" than "self," making them more steady in their habits but much less available. Getting the next gig is more a matter of tilting at windmills than dashing to battle or sailing for the New World.) The freelancer has a lot of time for dating—or no time. It is always feast or famine, and that goes for the pocket as well. I haven't mentioned money in the trifecta of graying Mystery Dates because freelancers (as I know all too well) rarely know what their income will be in six months and are too often asking (and re-asking) for money owed. We have every good quality except for predictability, solvency and a tolerance for panty hose.

. . .

The decision to actually go out on a date (i.e., meet and talk) is based on a complicated trading game of résumés in which cachet is based on how many O-Pee-Chee 1968 New York Mets cards I have versus how many Topps 1963 Cincinnati Reds he's holding.

Is he holding a redundant Eddie Kasko or a knocked-around Pete Rose?

Let me break it down for you.

I'm not mixer material for *The Millionaire Matchmaker.* On the one hand, my income level and weight should probably have me dating men who are more familiar with wet cement than adjectives, but on the other, a potential date can Google my

prose and vitae for hours. Then again, I swing between teaching freshman composition on an adjunct basis and walking dogs
to make my advances meet.

I may be fat, but I'm cute. I have good legs, great hair, a big
smile and pretty eyes. It's not hard to see past my weight. Yes,
I live in the Bat Cave, but it's in one of the best neighborhoods
in the five boroughs.

What all those subordinating conjunctions mean is that I'm
holding a Ryan Nolan, but its condition is questionable.

Guys, being guys, rate themselves on the stuff they think
they're looking *for*, on Eddie Kosko or Pete Rose, irrespective
of team or season. He thinks that being fit, having a sense of
humor, being "professional," enjoying "fine dining" and being
"real" is what he wants from a woman and therefore what he
thinks a woman wants from him. Most of the time, guys think
those buzzwords have meaning. Most of the time, they don't.

My friend Ellen, just leaving her fifties, is one of the exceptions. She teaches French in one of the city's prep schools and,
after a full cycle of vaccines in being Life Coached through *A
Course in Miracles*, *The Artist's Way* and the complete works of
Deepak Chopra, she feels she is entitled to a man who has
retired on six figures and looks great in a tux.

Okay, maybe she's not my friend. That entitlement thing kind
of ruined my respect for her. I can't write a book pitched to *The
Real Housewives of Anywhere* because of the overwhelming need some
women have for the right men to make them the right women.

The good news is that, mostly, men don't really want *the*
card, they want *a* card, and most women are exactly the same

way. We're all pretty much looking for someone nice and someone sensible whose baggage can be wedged into the overhead compartment.

I say it's good news because I got extra points I wasn't counting on when I wrote that craigslist ad. My weight was less important than the experts say it is.* My subsistence as a writer/ dog walker/adjunct professor was something of an asset because it meant I could stay out late or meet for lunch on Bayard Street. Sometimes a Mr. Extension 6651 got to flatter himself for daring to date someone so kicky.

I exchanged a few emails with a guy named Moshe. He, too, was a drifting professor, although he didn't tell me whether this meant he adjuncted around or had a full-time position at one of the Drop-Out Factory colleges—for-profits in which anyone with a loan can pretend, until they get their first homework assignment, they're going to get a degree.

I couldn't tell whether he had acne or acne scarring or something he could brag about like rosacea; I am certain, however, that his open-at-the collar shirt was polyester. His hair was dishwater, as were his eyes.

As was the rest of his complexion.

Nonetheless, it seemed worth scratching at his surface since we both taught international students and we both lived in

---

* "No need to despair if your hourglass figure has gained half an hour," Shirley Friedenthal and Howard Eisenberg chirp in *It's Never Too Late to Date*. "It's never too late to lose weight."

Brooklyn. He was into "interesting desserts," whatever that meant, which prodded me to explain I was being pretty rigorous about sticking to my diet.

Then he asked what I thought of his photo. Why do these guys always want to know what I think when they send their photo?

I thought he looked like a mouth-breather. I thought it was possible that he became a professor because he'd been turned down by parking cop school. I thought he looked like a guy who had a wankerchief and couldn't get off if it wasn't right there.

I thought he looked like a guy who *always* had his Wanky Blankie with him.

"Nice smile," I responded.

"How much weight do you want to lose?" he shot back.

Whoa, cowschlump! I thought as I sat back in my chair. He was quickly running through my collection of polite clichés. I needed at least a day to formulate a response.

"Dunno," I finally wrote.

In less than five minutes I had an invitation. "Do you want to have coffee at Junior's tonight?"

I had dogs to walk, I told him. Maybe another night.

How many dogs?

If I had told him I couldn't go because I had to breathe, he'd have asked how many breaths. I deleted the email, figuring he'd get it that our brief exchange wasn't progressing.

Clue: If he wants to know if you think he's cute, he's not going away.

Heading into the next weekend I got another email asking if we were going to get together or not. I hate being the dumper almost as much as being the dumpee but had had a few days to recover my niceness.

"I seem to be busier than I thought I was," I wrote carefully. "Maybe this is not the time for me to date. But you're smart and have a great job—you'll be a babe magnet!"

My mother would have been proud.

Moshe's mother, however, would have thought I was being a shiksa basmalke. "If you lose more weight this summer, maybe you'll be a guy magnet," he responded.

A huge shiver overtook me. That was an ego that would definitely have to be checked at the gate.

•   •   •

In the end, I was finding craigslist to be a fabulous source of insults, some obvious and others crafty in the way they led to sabotage. I deleted more liberally and my attention drifted to other things—photographing irises and trying to catalogue (and failing, alas, for another year) the scent of each kind, reading essays I could assign students whose first language ranged from Blanglish* to Nigerian to Danish, and trying to figure out the 1,800 dating websites that promised me true love.

Which is, of course, when the last possible candidate responded on the last day of the ad.

---

* New York City Black and/or Spanish patois: "I been axin' a' the bookstore but day don' 'ave it."

Four

Wild moose are well known to attempt to
have sex with domestic horses.

He got me by using the word "adaptive" in his first email.

In case you're a wonderful man reading this and want to
know how to seduce me, I'm a sucker for the slightly unusual,
correctly used, succulently pronounced single word. My knees
have literally gone weak at the words "apoplectic" and "Luddite."

I was so struck by "adaptive" that I didn't notice the context:
"I'm passionate, affectionate, adaptive, attentive." If I had, I
certainly would have asked what the hell all that added up to.

My lack of questions with Paul has turned into the most
heavily researched chapter of this book.

He offered himself up in the subject line—"You've Got
Male!"—and followed up with a résumé: Ivy League, on the
staff of his undergraduate humor magazine and a stint as a
stand-up, attorney for the city, memberships with the Brooklyn

Botanic Garden and the city zoos. I'm always a little skeptical when Jewish men come knocking, but he was divorced and nearly my age. Maybe, I thought, the pressure to keep it kosher eases up after a marriage and fatherhood are checked off one's list of things to do.

Please give me back my naïveté, God. The start of my season of dating was already starting to age me unnaturally.

．　．　．

In the second round of emails on that mid-May afternoon, he joked that I looked like Betsy Gotbaum, the ten-year New York City Public Advocate who didn't do a whole lot of anything from what I could tell. I didn't mind the comparison physically but, once again, who the hell is reminded of minor politicos?

Nerds, Frances. Very nerdy nerds.

I was also somewhat troubled by his enthusiasm for good "logistics" with women, which translated, in my case, into being one stop on his way home from his office. My idea of logistics is whether we can spend a weekend together a couple of times a year.

This is a point where age matters, although not so much as in how old we are but when we grew up. Paul's photo showed smiling eyes, almost all of his hair and a copious beard. I didn't think much about the beard, partly because it got lost in the dark suit in his head shot, but mostly because I graduated from a college-town high school in 1975. In those days I fell asleep to Cat Stevens singing "Wild World." It didn't matter that, in

2010, I didn't want to dress up like Carole King anymore. I sneer at the hippie moms in the neighborhood for living in million-dollar co-ops but never getting a proper haircut. Somehow, though, I didn't realize that none of the men I saw around my neighborhood looked like they'd stepped off the *Abbey Road* album cover (including the husbands of the hippie moms).

I thought he was handsome enough. Maybe I thought if we went out that I'd encourage him to trim things a bit or maybe I was having an acid flashback to Emerson, Lake and Palmer. Whatever. I clearly wasn't thinking whether he looked in any way like other lawyers in New York City.

Actually, I told him later that day, he looked a little like Charles Manson.

"Arrr'm not Charrr-les Manson," he said when he called. He approached speech like a pirate reading an unfamiliar script. I'd never heard such a lack of affect before. If you hooked his vocal chords up to an EKG, he'd flatline.

"That's reassuring," I answered.

Silence hung like rain on the New Jersey horizon.

"So . . . what're you up to this weekend?" I asked desperately.

"Synagogue tonight and tomorrow. I have my children on Sunday."

"Ah." What was I supposed to say to this? "You observe the Sabbath, then." *(Brilliant, Frances.)*

"I'm pretty observant."

"No Friday night movies, then."

"Not really, no."

The silence had a 40 percent chance of sudden heavy rainfall in parts of Long Island.

"What are you doing this weekend?" he asked.

I was making my Famous Pea Salad for a cookout at Ben and Jean's—raw cauliflower, peas, red onion, sour cream, mayonnaise, cheddar cheese and about a pound of bacon. I cleared my throat and said, "Having dinner with friends."

I didn't know if I was really communicating with this man with no vocal inflections who described jokes instead of telling them, but I knew that Orthodox Shabbat meant he'd be as good a date on weekend nights as a boyfriend who worked a round-trip flight to Liaoning Province. I put him in the back of my mind and more or less forgot about him.

He, on the other hand, felt we'd "made good small talk." Monday morning's email then went on to describe a *Far Side* cartoon about extraterrestrials putting a man and a bear in the same terrarium. "This week I'm busy with a friend who is visiting from Seattle, plus a Jewish holiday on Wednesday and Thursday (I won't be calling and emailing then)," he finished, but maybe we could meet after that.

"Happy holiday," I emailed back, and fluffed him off again. I was doing research, perusing other dating sites on the Net and in contact with various men.

He appreciated my holiday wishes enough to write that he came from a non-religious family but became observant in college, adding, "I don't care about a woman's religion and tend to date non-Jewish women since for some reason they're more accepting of my observance. In fact my last girlfriend was an ex-nun."

The ex-nun caused me a severe case of the heebie-jeebies. The thought of sharing, even at a remove, the Giving Tree with Sister Mary Anybody had me shaking in the confessional.

If that wasn't creepy enough, why would a gentile be more tolerant of his devoutness? And why didn't he care what my religion is? *I* care about my religion. I think it's rich and gory and pagan and criminal and hilarious. Given my druthers, if I'm going to date a guy my age, I'd prefer he be a Catholic because we share a history that for the most part ended with the baby boomers. No forty-year-old will laugh over a childhood of moving over in his seat to make room for his guardian angel or know the exhilaration of being seven years old and voting whether to name their first pagan baby Charbel or Isidore. When the going got tough, wouldn't Paul want the default conversation he could have with a woman who could recite the ten plagues the way we tot up reindeer or the seven deadly sins? When the silence turned black, wouldn't it be easier to be with a chick who has stories like the time Uncle Galil hid the Passover afikomen in Bubbe's favorite armchair, thus cheating all the kids out of their ransom prize?

I had agreed to this diet of dating partly because of how much I hated Saturday nights. It was May. Saturday night didn't *begin* until almost nine o'clock.

I'd never really learned how to date around—go to a movie with Harry on Tuesday, take in the American Wing at the Met with Jack on Friday, play Frisbee and grab a bite with Ted on Saturday, then repeat in a different order and different venues but with the same men.

Paul could be my reason to learn.

• • •

I decided I'd better get a closer look at the polar bear in the terrarium. I called Bette.

"How do you pronounce Shŏv-you-ought?"

"Shove-who?"

"Didn't you go to yeshiva? It's this spring holiday you guys have."

"We have a million of them, Franny. Almost as many as you guys." Bette likes to spring Catholic holy days on me. I'd scored serious street cred from acing the Assumption the summer before.

"C'mon, Bette. Moses got the Commandments? The guys stay up reading the Bible all night? It's like New York News One: all-Torah-all-the-time. *Shŏv-you-ought.*"

"We pronounce it Shŏv-you-ought. Why do you want to know?"

"I've been talking to this guy. He's, like, really Jewish."

"What's his name?"

"Paul."

"Paul."

"Yeah. Like Paul the Apostle. Wrote the Epistles in the New Testament. Maybe his middle name is Schlomo."

"Paul the *musernik.** Innnt-errr-esting." Her exaggeration

---

* Google is good at translating my wild misspellings. A *musernik* is a student of Jewish morals and ethics.

meant I had her rapt attention, and she only hauled out her Yiddish for good reason. "Keep me posted."

*   *   *

Will would have been in fits at this point. When I was in eighth grade my mother and I took the train from Missoula to Portland, Oregon. We sat down in our scratchy Northern Pacific seats and she handed me a copy of Chaim Potok's *The Chosen*. I didn't speak another word until I had to greet my grandparents the next day.

I've always been enchanted by a long dress and a couple of archaisms. Add a chemise and a bonnet and I'm good to go. It was 1970 and I couldn't believe no one had told me there were people living in the eighteenth century. I announced that I didn't want to be confirmed in the Catholic Church because I intended to convert to Hassidic Judaism as soon as I could find a Hassidic Jew to do it.

My father was not amused.

In fact he gave me a clear choice: Be confirmed and he'd never make me go to Mass again, or else find someplace else to live.

My confirmation name is Bernadette, and I didn't go to church for anything except weddings or funerals until I was in college and fell in love with a priest.

By the time I actually met some Jews, in graduate school, I had long ago relinquished my dream of having babies while my husband twirled his peyos and dreamed of Maimonides. I realized

East Coast Jews really are different from Montana Catholics and that I didn't give a rat's ass about summer camp and arguing for the sake of arguing. I do, however, feel that Jews, Catholics and Baptists make the best writers because we live in a sea of broken thou-shalt-nots.

Will has never let me forget my years of wanting to convert. It's funnier than Yiddish to him and we both find Yiddish hysterically funny.

"Glad you like Yiddish," Paul said when I told him of my fondness for the language. "Ever notice how practically all the insulting terms start with a 'sch' (shlemeil, shlemazel, schmuck, etc.)?"

He forgot to include shiksa.

. . .

I was not clicking with Paul-guy, but after Sol and the Orange Rose Guy, his willingness to get to know me was refreshing. Also, he had the luck or ability to touch upon just enough Yiddishkeit that I always had to reply. When, for example, I mentioned that Kuffel is Polish, he topped me by mentioning both that his people were a polyglot of Eastern Europeans and that if it was probable that I didn't like Polish jokes, did I like Jewish jokes?

I could only groan.

If the mention of a tin can reminded him of a *Far Side* cartoon or *Simpsons* episode, Jewish heritage always reminds me of a boss who, in the first week I worked for her, was nattering on about her Jewish ancestors in the seventeenth century. She stopped and looked at me. "I forgot to ask you, Frahn-ces. What was *your* family doing in the seventeenth century?"

I didn't yet know this woman from Adam and without thinking I answered, "Well, Barbara, in the seventeenth century my people were busy killing your people."

The expression on her face defined the word "askance."

"I love priest/rabbi jokes and I had a whole collection of Jesus jokes at one time," I wrote back, and added, "Easterners don't really tell jokes, at least not like Westerners. We use them as a substitute for conversation."

Which summoned this joke:

"Person Number One: I've got a joke for you. Two Jews . . .

"Person Number Two: Stop! Why does it always have to be two Jews? Why can't it be two Albanians or two Swiss or two Zulus?

"Person Number One: Okay. Two Zulus were standing at the back of a synagogue . . ."

•   •   •

It was going on a month after my *Looking for Mr. Goodbar* debacle, and I hadn't gone out with anyone else. I figured I should meet Paul and check out the chemistry in person. He couldn't have been more blatant. Along with the right logistics of where I lived, he wanted to find "someone before the summer with whom to start a relationship," which felt like ordering a hamburger, but I was going into all of this with an open mind. I've fallen in love at first sight and I've fallen in love after knowing a man a long time. After much back-and-forthing, we finally set a lunch date. I wasn't thrilled about going to House of Tofu (I like meat), but it was certified kosher.

And he sent me two articles about Montana Jews. Each featured a Lubavitcher rabbi.

How . . . strange, I thought. Every New Yorker knows Lubavitchers on sight, the fedora-wearing, bearded, black-suited men with their Chanukah mobiles rumbling through the streets making sure there is a menorah in every home and vodka in every campus Chabad outreach house.

I couldn't imagine Lubavitchers in Whitefish, Montana. They must all migrate for Passover because I'd bet my life there wasn't a piece of matzo between there and Minneapolis. And where did they get meat and milk???

One of the articles came from a website called crownheights .info. Its ads flash with blinding speed for brises, shtender stores, professional kosher cooking schools and—*holy frugivore shit, Batman!*—*psychotherapist matchmakers.* What does it say that this is part of his reading material?

I'm noddingly acquainted with Lubavitchers. They own and run my favorite office supply store six blocks from my house. The young ones at the registers are funny and breezy and barricaded behind their high counter. The older ones in the back scowl perpetual questions at customers. *You don't* really *want a Xerox of that, do you? Why do you need an office chair?* Every New Yorker knows why the attitudes and the barricades are up:

*And if a woman have an issue, and her issue in her
flesh be blood, she shall be put apart seven days: and
whosoever toucheth her shall be unclean until the
even. . . . And whosoever toucheth any thing that she
sat upon shall wash his clothes, and bathe himself
in water, and be unclean until the even.**

No woman in Brooklyn would dream of trying to shake hands
with a man with peyos. We are, as a gender, unclean.

But what else was involved with dating a member of one of
the Twelve Tribes? The Saturday before lunch, I curled up with
Daisy and the Old Testament. When it comes to sex, everything
was there in the Pentateuch. No adultery, no sex before marriage, no bestiality, no homosexuality, no incest, no ejaculation
anywhere besides your wife's sausage wallet.†

One could expect anything from death by stoning to expul-
sion from the tribe for committing one of these, um, acts. My
apologies to Moses, but I can't go along with the word "abom-
inations" for a few of these choices.

The news wasn't good for the ecumenical couple either.

---

* Leviticus 15:19–23.

† Now if someone could explain to me exactly why the Christian Right
gets to use Leviticus to condemn homosexuality while lunching on crab-
stuffed pork and steamed cormorant, I might give up the Big Bang and
be saved.

> *. . . we have forsaken thy commandments, Which thou has*
> *commanded by thy servants the prophets, saying, The land,*
> *unto which you go to possess it, is an unclean land with*
> *the filthiness of the people of the lands, with their abomina-*
> *tions* [read: my abominations], *which have filled it*
> *from one end to the other with their uncleanness. . . . there-*
> *fore let us make a covenant with our God to put away all*
> *the wives, and such as are born to them . . .**

So if doing the naughties with your Jewish *wife* has an infinity of
restrictions and the Old Testament prophets happily banished the
half-Jewish kids—the Gershom—from hearth and home, how
could Paul possibly justify a goyishe girlfriend? Wouldn't he be
sinning all the way to the Catskills and back with this defilement?

•   •   •

How do you dress for your first date with a big-time Orthodox
Jew? Am I supposed to wear tights? A hat? A *wig*? What would
be considered disrespectful? I think about what nuns in civvies
wear and figure that would probably be about right, so I brush
my hair, put on black jeans and an airy—which is to say,
transparent—pink linen shirt. With a royal blue bra. You want
shiksa, I tell the blue eyes looking back at me in the mirror, I'll
give you shiksa.

---

* Ezra 9:10–10:3.

It's no mystery which man coming into the House of Tofu is Paul. That would be the guy in the straw fedora, knotted fringes flying and a beard broad enough for us to picnic on.

The head shot had not shown how shaggy his beard was, but I couldn't just blurt out, "What's with the haystack on your chin?" If the *frum** who sell the only pens I can write with are clean-shaven, why can't he be? I wondered.† Kissing . . . *that* . . . would scrape my face raw.

We order quickly and sip our musty Chinese tea. My mouth is dry, as it always is on a first date. I want a diet Coke and a cigarette. Badly.

Paul has Googled me and has questions about my past. I squirm under the interrogation. I am tired of myself; it goes with the territory of writing memoirs. It occurs to me as he asks about my romantic history that one reason it would be nice to have a boyfriend is so that I'd be so otherwise-directed that I could stop thinking and writing about me-me-me all the time.

"Arrr-nd have your books sold well?" he asks.

"The first did; the last not so much."

"How many copies?"

---

* *Frum*, which means "pious" in Yiddish, refers to Orthodox Jews. Really Orthodox Jews are known as *frummers*.

† As I learned later, Leviticus is the Boy Scout manual for what to wear, what to eat, who to fuck and how to pray. Orthodox Jews shave their beards off when they are in mourning but otherwise observe the commandment, ". . . neither shalt thou mar the corner of thy beard" (Leviticus 19:27).

I shrug and look wildly for a waiter bearing tofu. "I don't really know. I don't think it would be good for me to know."

"Rrrrr-eminds me of a joke. One gentile says, 'How's your shop doing?' and the second one says, 'Great! Thanks for asking.'"

There would be time to go sauté my own string beans in the silence.

"You don't think that's funny?"

"Uh, sure." *The art of conversation is in being a good listener,* my mother always told me.

"Bee-caws if it was two *Jews*, the second one would say, "We haven't gone out of business yet, p'ttt, p'ttt, *kneina hura.*"

Tiny bubbles of spittle remain on his lips. I stare at him, fascinated, then push the bottle of soy sauce toward him. "There's no salt on the table. Maybe you can toss this over your shoulder."

"That could hurt someone."

"Not the bottle, the sauce. At most you'll have to pay dry cleaning."

"Ha, ha, ha."

It's genuine appreciation, but that's what he says: *ha, ha, ha.*

"Did you like the articles I sent you?" he asks before digging into his shiny scarlet sauce–covered glop.

"Yes, although Lubavitchers in Montana is not the Montana I grew up in." I spear a green bean. "Both of those articles are about Lubavitchers. Are you a Lubavitcher?"

He sits back in his chair and regards me for a moment before saying, slowly, "I *know* the Lubavitchers . . ."

Jaysus, Mary and Joseph, I think. He "knows" them?

"But you date shiksas."

"No Jewish woman would have me."

I look at the other people in the restaurant, a couple of Gen X moms talking with their chopsticks, two mail carriers, an older man absorbed in a book. They're all having themselves a party while I'm in purgatory. Do Jews believe in purgatory?

We bump haltingly through the meal and after we pay the bill, he stands to let me go out first.

"This was fun," he says when we were out on the street. "We should do it again."

"Sure. Soon." I start to reach out to shake hands but pull back. I'm rolling right along through the last of a fairly eventless menopause, but I'm not mikvehed or absolved or anything.

I stop at the newsstand across the street to buy a soda, walk over to sit in Jean and Ben's garden and tell her about the big date. I describe his flat voice and some of the other men I've met or am talking to while I smoke my way back to feeling normal.

"You know nothing can happen with him, right?" she says.

"Yeah. But it's interesting research."

"Or would be, if he was interesting."

When I get home an hour later there is an email waiting. "Since your ad was only a head shot, I took a few glances in order to check out and admire your physique. I apologize if you found that too obvious."

I hadn't noticed. I'm too nervous on a first date to tune in to men's reactions to me, all that body language stuff that *Cosmo* promises will let a gal psych the guy out before he's asked her last name. It was nice that he approved and that he apologized, but . . .

* * *

I called Bette.

"Will you be offended if I call this guy the Jew Boy?"

There was another one of those silences bearing down the telephone at me.

"Why would you want to do that?" she asked cautiously.

"He tucks his peyos behind his ears. When I asked him if he was a Lubavitcher, he said, 'I . . . know the Lubavitchers.'"

"No, you cannot call him the Jew Boy. That's an offense to Jews. He's the Big Fat Jew Boy."

"But he's not fat." I laughed.

"It doesn't matter. Did he have tzizit?"

"Hard to tell with that much beard."

She groaned. "Not acne, Franny. But don't tell me he has a beard? Did his food get stuck in it?"

"He was neat and clean from what I could tell. Except for the beard."

"And the tzizit? Fringes?"

"Oh, yeah," I drawled. "He had fringes."

"Then he's a Big Fat Jew."

* * *

I thought Bette was being cruel for the sake of hilarity until Daisy and I ran into our neighbors, Carol and Celia, making the sundown circuit with Hazard and Pooh, their shepherd mix dogs and Daisy's good friends.

"So I had lunch with this guy yesterday," I said as I fell into step with them. Celia extracted a cigarette as we passed out of view of their apartment building and the vigilant eyes of her ten-year-old daughter. "He's a divorced Orthodox Jew. When I asked him why he wanted to date a goy, he said no Jewish woman would go out with him."

Carol shrieked. "No shit, Sherlock! And you can't either. I like you too much."

"But there must be plenty of divorced or widowed Jewish women who would love to bag themselves a lawyer."

Carol and Celia exchanged looks. The kind of looks you exchange when you haven't told the other person she has pancreatic cancer. Yet.

"Tell us more," Celia said. I love Celia's voice. It has the clean, clear resonance of a bell. It's no wonder she's a hotshot lawyer for a city agency for the elderly. People would tell her anything.

"I don't know much more than that. He has two kids who are going away to summer camp in a couple of weeks so he dates in the summer. I asked him if he was a Lubavitcher and he said no but he 'knows' them. He's a lawyer with the city but I don't know for what."

"Probably a tax lawyer," Carol said dryly.

"I went to Cardozo School of Law," Celia said. "My class was full of yeshiva boys. They could argue night into day and still want to twist the sun into something else."

"I didn't know you went to Cardozo," Carol said. "I figured you went back home in Ohio."

"No, that's how I came to New York."

"Oh . . . I actually went to Boston College. That was pretty wild, a Jewish girl among the Jesuits."

"You must have killed them," Celia said.

"I liked it, but I couldn't wait to get to New York. Where is this guy from, Frances?"

"Baltimore. He didn't become observant until college."

Both women sighed an exaggerated "oh."

"A BT,"* Carol said knowingly. "They're the worst kind."

"I hope you didn't wear slacks to lunch," Celia said, her eyes crinkling up in laughter.

"Or a linen and wool blend," Carol added.

I looked from one to the other. "I don't get it. He wore a hat to lunch. He has the beard and the peyos and the fringes and disappeared for Shavuot, which I still can't pronounce. Why would he want to date a shiksa when there are a million rules I'm going to break just by breathing?"

"Six hundred and thirteen of them, actually," Celia said.

"Get it?" Carol asked.

"Get what?" I was completely bewildered.

"Of course no Jewish woman will go out with him. Who wants to deal with all those laws? And besides, the beard. Yuck."

"Ugh," Celia concurred. "They're all so—"

---

* Baal Teshuva: a Jew who has become observant rather than being born into orthodoxy.

"*Clumpy*," Carol said.

"And if he's a Lubavitcher—"

"Arrogant," Carol filled in. "They give me the willies."

"But you guys are Jewish!"

"Oh, Frances." Celia crinkled. "Didn't you know no one hates Jewishy Jews more than other Jews?"

"At least the frummies," Carol said. "Woof."

Daisy, Pooh and Hazard looked up at that. Pooh pawed my shin and Daisy and Hazard began asking very loudly for cookies.

• • •

It was my psychiatrist, Dr. Roseblatt, whose MD is from another Yeshiva University school, the Albert Einstein College of Medicine, who was most horrified.

"A Black Hat??? You can't go out with a Black Hat, Frances. They're horrible. I interned at Beth Israel and when I walked by them I could *feel* their eyes drilling into me. I'm blonde so they didn't know I'm Jewish. It was like a field day for ogling."

I was so amused by my psychiatrist's reaction that I emailed it to Carol. "Big hats have little yelmeke," she responded.

I began teaching summer quarter not long after lunch with Paul. There were other guys I was seeing and/or flirting with, and the lack of a weekend date night was counter to my purposes in dating. I suggested we might not be a match.

And yet I remain fixated on the puzzle of Paul. Perhaps I

should be grateful for the do-si-do of the few weeks we communicated. Because of him, I've ended up reading more of the Old Testament than I did for my bachelor's degree in religious studies. I have come to admire a great deal of the joy and tenaciousness that are the story of Hasidic Jewry, and I've come to see how much of Catholicism's ritual and canon are derivations from its Judaic roots. I continue to be suspicious that Paul was looking for sex, but sex based on conversation is the least of what I'm looking for and all too rare at that.

Convinced that there is some Halachic loophole that would allow sex with a gentile without stoning or a good strong bath, my research into the interstices of rules governing relations with gentiles led to a phone call to Rabbi Simon Jacobson, a bestselling author and founder of the Meaningful Life Center, a Torah-centered "spiritual Starbucks" (which, I guess, means drop in for ten minutes of Torah and lattè) but after he scoffed at the idea of a sexual exemption ("No one is perfect. Observant Jews sin as much as anyone."), he went on to interview *me*. It might have been a chance for him to dig in to my world a little, although he found, when I told him I'm fifty-four and never married, that I am not a typical secular gentile.

"Do you mind me asking all these question?"

"Not at all," I said. Anyone can find the answers to his questions by reading my books or blogs, but I felt somehow that I was in the presence of someone prayerful and authentic and, maybe, holy.

"Did you ever find your birth mother?"

"No. I was never really interested," I told him. "I figure the people who changed my diapers and paid for graduate school are my real parents."

"Ah. But what if"—his voice dropped to a whisper—"she's *Jewish*? That would make *you* a Jew."

Yeah. Me and the king of Denmark.

Five

The male bowerbird incorporates hundreds of
brightly colored objects in his nest, including
shells, flowers, feathers, stones, berries, plastic
garbage, coins, nails, rifle shells or pieces of glass.
He spends hours grooming his collection, which
reflects his ability to procure items from his
habitat. He often steals from neighbors.

I cannot overstate what a bumbler I am when it comes to dating.

With exactly two exceptions, every boyfriend, lover or crush
I've had in the last ten years has started with me having an
almost neutral opinion. Affection may take me a day or it may
take a couple of months, but in the beginning, if we are in any
way suited, I reserve judgment.

Perhaps a better way to put this is that I leave the judgment
up to the guy and I go along with it.

My passivity is born of inexperience and a frightfully low
opinion of myself. I am not, however, a sucker.

Much.

. . .

At first Bette was enthusiastic.

"Ooh," she said when I forwarded his profile to her. "He's cute. I like that boyish thing with the graying hair. I wonder what kind of restaurant the photo was taken in."

"I think he's cute, too. But he's four years younger than me."

She snorted. "Like that's ever stopped you. Look, Franny. He went to Johns Hopkins. He's a gardener. You guys are, like, perfect."

Danny was certainly enthusiastic in his first email. He liked weekends in Paris and was the owner of "an interesting and financially successful business which provides me with freedom."

On the other hand, his profile was fluent but his email was a grammatical mess, which I couldn't square with weekends in Paris. I mean, those are long enough flights to read a lot of books and magazines. Even if they were *Popular Mechanics* and schlocky thrillers, some of the grammar should rub off. And he lived in Florida. I was tired of long-distance relationships. It made me think that Paul's logistics of the Lexington Express wasn't such a bad idea.

In for a penny, however, in for a pound. "You live in Florida!" I wrote back. "How can we make that work? You will have to fall very madly in love with me and move me down, I suppose."

I mean, what the hell? I could toss my hair and act imperious while indulging fantasies of living barefoot among the herb borders with this man I hadn't yet spoken to who seemed to be on me like white on rice.

But then again, why was such a guy on Ashley Madison? It's not exactly the kind of place where gardening is a skill to brag about.

Ashley Madison guarantees that its paying members will have an affair. I didn't fork over my Visa number so there was no promise that I'd be looking for my high heels, but I hope to God those pictures will never be found by a houseguest.

I'd posted a terse profile there in a fit of revenge. Every other month or so, I Google men I once loved (you do too, so stop rolling your eyes). Eric, the man who broke my heart a couple of years ago, was hacking endlessly away at a book proposal to rewrite Gay Talese's *Couples* for the new millennium. Despite the presence of a girlfriend on Myspace and Facebook, he said on his website that he was up for anything.

Anything??? I screeched at my computer screen. I have had a hell of a time letting go of Eric, largely because there are writerly and comic things about me that he won't let go. But one of the things I've used to delete his emails was a conversation in which he admitted he found sex with me to be too vanilla.

Funny that when he mentioned that, it was what I automatically thought about sex with him.

Up for anything, my, er, foot.

That was all I needed to find the naughty photos a boyfriend once took of me and post them while whistling the tune of "Anything You Can Do."

Hell, Eric, hath no fury. You didn't bring out my dark side, but by now I've learned how to do it myself. If my Ashley Madison profile was a secret revenge, it still felt sweet.

But what was a guy who "like[s] dogs and children" doing on a dating site populated with user names like Tuff&Ruff?

"My daughter made me put up a personal," he wrote back. "I didn't know Ashley Madison is like that."

Did I believe him? No. Ten minutes on Ashley Madison is enough to make you want to wash your hands with bleach. I sat back and tried to imagine a daughter writing his ad and him posting it on Ashley Madison. But I liked what I'd read and decided I'd kid him about it for the rest of our lives.

He was a widow, he wrote soon after, with a fourteen-year-old who attended the Florida Air Academy. "Just like her mother," he said proudly. "She's determined to fly."

Danny, too, was flying . . . to France on a business trip. He called me for the first time as he was driving to the airport. The static on his cell phone made him sound like we were playing mermaids, but I was able to make out that he'd be in meetings for a few days and hence unavailable. "Kiss, kiss," he signed off through the bubbles and eddies. I liked that. I know a couple of Brits who say that.

· · ·

The next I heard from him he had been awarded a huge decorating contract for the government of Benin. Benin! I opened my atlas, hoping it was a small island in the French West Indies or a region of France I hadn't heard of before.

I got the French part right. It's a former colony, resting six degrees above the equator on the Atlantic in West Africa. Three of its border countries are among three of thirty-three countries on the State Department's Travel Warnings list and another seven nations on that list are within a two-hour flight from Cotonou, the coastal city where Danny was working (or not working). American travelers are warned against crowds and walking alone on the beach at any time of day. The primary industry is subsistence farming. Its secondary industry is scamming gullible American women into taking out cash on their credit cards.

"Cool," Ben said. "Have him send me stamps."

Danny was in the *Heart of Darkness* and I found myself corresponding with his daughter, Hellie, who was delighted to have a new "Ma" and "a funny dog" in her life.

Ma?????

I answered that I was a long ways away from being her mum and that she wrote in the same scattershot fashion as her father. Then I forwarded this batch of emails to Bette.

"Don't do this, Fran," she said as soon as I picked up the phone. "It's a scam."

"I know," I said. "But isn't it delicious?"

"No. It's stupid and I don't want you to get hurt."

"I'm not gonna get hurt, silly. I just wanna know what he wants."

"Who *cares*?" she snapped. "He's trying to sucker you in."

"Bette." I wanted to slow her sudden prickliness down. "Bette. Don't you think it's, I don't know, interesting? I mean, you hear about this stuff and now it's happening. I want to see it play out."

"You're clinging to the idea that he's in love with you."

"No, I'm not!" I was starting to get angry now, too, in that way that happens when someone doesn't see the humor in a situation.

"I can't talk about this, Frances. I'm afraid for you. Talk about something else. How's Daisy?"

So I backed off and told her about walking Daisy and her best friend, Hero, an inscrutable white Lab and one of my favorite dogs ever. That morning she had taken umbrage at a beagle named Bacchus and whipped me 180 degrees around in sheer fury. My left shoulder and arm were killing me. I was looking forward to starting to teach so my body could heal from six years of walking Labradors who lunged for invisible bread crumbs and sudden enemies. It had been six years of suppurating wounds, green bruises, stress fractures, lower back pain and more love than a single human being deserves.

"Bacchus," she cooed. "I love that dog. When you see that dog again, tell him I'm gonna come suck his brains out his ears." Bette knew every dog in the Heights and had walked most of them in her years as a much more successful walker than I had ever wanted to be.

"Daisy used to hate him, too," I said. "One day I gave her a cookie to make her behave, and then I gave him the other half. They did the butt-sniff Maypole and have been friends ever since."

"I'm gonna come suck *her* brains out, too. Make her do the Thing."

It's a slightly cruel trick I play on Daisy that tickles Bette into threats of further canine dining. I call out, "Hello? Hello?" as if someone is outside my door and Daisy starts barking her own greetings.

"She's such a fluffer-nutter," Bette said through the commotion. I sat down to comfort Daisy, who promptly flipped over for a belly rub, looking at me flirtatiously. "Who else are you talking to besides the so-called Danny Foster?"

"I've put profiles up on a bunch of different sites. I actually paid for eHarmony. What a rip-off. You take this big personality test and then they send you your potential dates. You don't get to do any boy-shopping at all."

"Who have they sent you?"

"A bunch of men whose most important accomplishments and favorite hobbies are their grandchildren."

"And you paid them *money* for this?"

"It's research, Bette. Tax write-off."

"Sometimes I'm glad I'm married," she said.

We said good-bye amiably, but I wondered why she didn't trust that I knew there was a lot of fishiness in Danny's stories.

• • •

A day or two later, I called my cell phone carrier so I could get transatlantic service. I knew it was going to be expensive calling Benin but I shrugged it off as another tax expense and gritted my teeth.

"It's so hot here," he complained. "I'm working twenty hours a day. I'll send you pictures. Also, something else, for your eyes only. I can't wait to come home to you."

I sat in my kitchen and smoked as I eked this out of the crackle of the Atlantic as it warmed and readied for hurricane season. When I asked him where he was staying, he said his employers had chosen badly and he wanted to move hotels.

Within hours he sent attachments. There were photos of a lighthouse set among rocks and pine trees; a kitchen paneled in pale oak with a vase of sunflowers on the island counter; chalet-type interior with a bearskin over the upstairs balustrade.

A white white living room with a merry fire in the hearth.

Are there sunflowers in Benin? Pine trees? Wouldn't merry puffs of air-conditioning be more appropriate?

And there was an Ecobank Benin draft made out to Danny Tommy Foster* for 5.5 million dollars. It looked suspiciously authentic.

It looked authentically suspicious.

"He either wants money, a green card or accommodation," Bette sighed. "Those pictures were lifted from a website."

I agreed and spent an eye-straining hour on Google Images trying phrases like "chocolate and white bedroom interior design" and "Danish modern dining table."

Chocolate bed linens were no longer popular.

"Give the Florida school a call," Bette challenged me. Hellie spent her early-June birthday alone and bereft of a cell phone, which she'd lost. Danny asked me to help her out but I answered with blithe firmness that, "I'm sure you could either give your credit card number to Hellie's headmaster or call whatever

---

* The "Tommy" was new. He'd used "Danny" with me.

carrier you're with and arrange to have a phone sent to Hellie. If you can call me, you can certainly do that."

Of course I knew there was no Hellie. I had no intention of spending the words trying to explain to the school why I was calling about her. And I wanted, badly, to see just how far he was going to go. Calling the school would end the experiment.

"I've decided he's for real," I gasped as soon as Bette picked up. "But he's a ventriloquist! He and Hellie can't write me at the same time."

"Uh-huh," she said.

"C'mon, Bette. Laugh," I wheedled. "All of these emails go into a folder named 'Scam,' you know. I'm not in love with this guy. I just want to know what his angle is."

That night it was Bette's turn to email me. "I'm sorry, Fran, but I feel Mr. Foster is not who he says he is. I won't be commenting on him any more. I support you, though, as always."

I whined to Daisy, "Well, that's no fun."

* * *

July and heat. Fifty freshman essays in piles on my desk. Other men I was seeing or talking to. There was a lull in communication with Danny, which I was not only grateful for but prolonged with a lie about having strep throat when he IM'd me with complaints about my end of the silence. He was sorely tried by the Beninese authorities as he tried to get his 5.5 million. He had to pay all the fees and taxes before he could withdraw it. He was eight thousand dollars short.

ing up.

I waited for him to ask for the money. He was cleverer than that. He'd lost both his phone and his Bible in a taxi. Would I send him a Bible?

Nice touch, I thought.

"Do you want a rosary, too?" I wrote back.

"Send it by DHL or FedEx. It will take 72 hours. Of course I'd be happy to have a rosary."

I sent him a link to the King James Bible online, to which he did not reply.

We definitely did not share a sense of irony.

An AT&T phone would be helpful, too, he added in instant messenger a few minutes later. He couldn't call me without it.

"I can't do that," I replied. "You have to get it in your name and make decisions about things. I won't put it in my name."

"Send it to 72 Pharmacy Shegbeya, Cotonou, Benin. The hotel manager will receive it for me—Mr. Oladiti Ezekiel."*

I said I'd look into it and promptly didn't.

I knew the combination of my recalcitrance and continued presence was acting like one of those fairy-tale irritants that made Rumplestiltskin tear himself in two. I also hoped to God that every other woman he was weaving this elaborate story for was as sadistic as I.

---

* Real addresses and real name. Or the ones he sent me. Sue me, Oladiti.

104

He cracked soon enough. Skipping like a stone across the waters of Benin's banking and treasury rules, he said his Internet connection was tenuous and so "we'd" better get to the point. "I have 67,100$ [sic] to come up with and I have raised 18,600. I have a travelers [sic] check of 35,000 that I can process by Monday. All i need to raise now is 13.5k. I don't mean to ask you this but I have tried all I could and [you are] all I am left with. Upon my arrival, I will REFUND it back, even with interest. I promise."*

I sat at my computer and laughed. "I don't have anything like the money you need."

"What do you have? I really need your help for the sake of US and our future, Hellie and Daisy."

"I have nothing, I'm sorry."

"It's okay. But I am crying . . . !"

Like Paul, I was reminded of a joke. How many Jewish mothers does it take to screw in a lightbulb?

"Never mind. I'll just sit here in the dark, all by myself . . ."

Coercing me to send the amount of taxes I myself owed the IRS turned to imperious demands for table scraps.

> *"Send $1250 by tomorrow. I am leaving as soon as I receive it. You can pick me up at the airport, then I can handle the rest. No argument. Just go and do it tomorrow."*

---

* Some grammar, punctuation and spelling have been fixed for your sanity.

"Yeah, right," I messaged back. "I have $1200 like I have a second head. This is not an argument. It's 'no,' plain as that."

It was tedious, this wheedling and guilt-tripping. I had the information I'd told Bette I wanted from him—he was out for money. I don't know why I kept up the pretense, except, perhaps, because I wanted to see if I could shame the gasbag grifter. *I* wanted to apply the thumbscrews. One night, I asked for his American address. He excused himself from instant messenger to take a business call (on what cell phone, exactly??), then sent me a Pensacola address. Zillow listed it as being for sale. It was a mess of weeds and cheap wood paneling, no pool or herb borders to go barefoot around.

"There are a lot of holes in your story," I emailed. "I don't think you live in Florida or have a daughter at FLAIR and I think that you've set this up to get money. I wish that wasn't true because despite how crappy it is that you'd do that, I quite enjoyed the fantasy."

"I understand you are thinking negative about me because I told you about my financial problem. Well sorry if I inconvinent you and I don't need your help in my situation," he snapped back.

"I want to see a scan of your passport," I replied. "I want to talk to Hellie. I want a scan of your driver's license. I know this is a scam, Danny."

"If you have someone else, just open up to me," he lamented. He wasn't good at this but I believe he'd studied up on Stockholm Syndrome. "When you see a scam, you will not know because they do things perfect and am not perfect because I am not a scammer. I [can] afford to feed you and your entire family for [the] next 20 year with what I have made in [Benin]."

Whatever. I sighed and went back to marking essays.

He tried once more, in August, to suck me in, with a complicated business in which I would be his beneficiary for funds transferred to my bank account. Instead of saying no, I made the mistake of saying it would have to be done through lawyers, which prolonged what was now simple tedium. After a few days of wrangling, he gave up. I breathed a sigh of relief that he'd tried me as far as he could and had gone away. I told Bette I'd finally scared him off. It was the first time she'd let me talk about him in two months.

"Congratulations," she said flatly and changed the subject to the weather, which was a heavy mass of sullen humidity along the eastern seaboard.

We finished dew points off in fifteen seconds and the discomfort of what she considered my Benin lunacy scratched to be brought up again.

"One of my students is Nigerian. I told him about Benin Boy. He said the problem is that there is an educated group of young people and no work for them to do. So they scam."

"Oh," she said. "Well, now you know. How's it going with the dating sites? Match, Zoosk—what else?"

I started laughing. "You'll love this. I got my daily matches from eHarmony the other day. Guess who one of them was? Eric! In a photo *I* took of him!"

"Good God," she said.

"You know he wants to write a book about sexual networking, right? Building some sort of orgiastic cult, I think, culled from the Net and strip joints." I laughed with as much genuine amusement as an executioner whetting his axe. "The only sex happening on eHarmony was his photo. I took it right after we'd had sex on his living room floor."

"Did you contact him?"

"No."

"Good."

"But I didn't delete it, either."

"Do you *look* for trouble or does it just come to you, like dog hair?"

"Right now I'm open to what happens, as long as it doesn't cost me any more money than a membership fee or a good date. But consider the irony, Bette. I posted a profile on Ashley Madison to one-up him and received his profile on marriage-minded eHarmony. Maybe we *were* meant for each other."

"Fran—"

"Just kidding. Besides, I one-upped him in the kinky sex department years ago. That's how I met Dar."

* * *

The thing about Romeo scammers is that as long as they have access to your email address, they will never go away. I took one demented misstep in my dealings with the Benin Bamboozler when I let him have my home address. One morning two weeks after Bette and I could relax and talk about anything again, I received a lovely, anonymous bouquet. I called the florist, who told me they were from Dan Foster but had no other information. I emailed my thanks and the next day he wrote to say a package was coming to my house, that it had a gift in it for me but that I should send the other contents on to him.

The first package arrived from a mail-order linen company. He had expensive taste. I was almost amused at the thought of a skinny black guy living in a Third World ghetto prancing around in his organic Turkish cotton, 400 grams per square meter weight bathrobe, air drying after a shower and an initial dry-off with his even heavier towel set. Total cost of freshening up: $353.90.

"I will give you the details to mail it when I get the shipping address," he responded to my notice of its arrival.

Five days later a big box came from Zappos, addressed care of Frances Kuffel.

I was pissed off. The Bat Cave is tiny. It cannot hold one thing more. The volume of those towels was equal to a couch and now I had a box to contend with.

"You gotta call the companies right *now*," Bette said. "He definitely used a stolen credit card and you are now holding stolen property. That's a felony, Frances." She sighed in exasperation. "Don't make me lose my respect for you."

An icy sweat broke out under my breasts and on my palms. "I didn't know I was endangering your respect."

"Just call the companies this shit came from, okay?"

Zappos confirmed it was a phony credit card and had UPS pick up the box the next day. I didn't open it; I had no interest in repacking stolen goods. The linen store said the charge had gone through without a problem.

"I'm going to hang on to the stuff," I told the manager, "and I'm emailing you my phone number. Please keep the email and be in touch if you find out differently."

I wrote "Danny" or whatever his name really was that he had used a stolen credit card and the game was up. Then I blocked him from email.

I knew he wouldn't spend the money to wheedle me back by phone and I felt reasonably safe that he wasn't going to show up at my door, although for the first time I was grateful that Daisy is the most prejudiced dog I've ever met.

At the end of September I got a phone call from the linen company. He'd used a stolen credit card number, which meant he'd scammed some woman into believing in his Johns Hopkins degree, affection for gardening, beautiful needy daughter and being stuck in Benin.

I mentioned the boxes to Tommy, the owner of the local UPS store. He told me that at least once a month, he has to call in the police because someone tries to send such care-of packages off to the Third World.

Bette was right. I thanked her for watching my back.

* * *

I came across at least a dozen scammers in wandering through Internet Date Land. There are websites devoted to outing Russian and African scammers, most of whom are men posing as either sex. The websites warn of consistent misspelling, crimes against grammar, web speak and a fetish for emoticons.* They're good signs except that as a teacher of composition, I know these mistakes are just as often made by Americans. All of the scams I came across used a variant of the guy being God-fearing as part of his self-description, and after a very brief exchange with "Steve" on OkCupid, I began to notify the website administrators each time I came across that phrase, along with other red signals. These include:

> *Being addressed as "Dear Pretty" (or "Beautiful" or some such) rather than by my profile name (which varies between an Evelyn Waugh and a Jane Austen character)*
>
> *Initial emails that react to nothing specific about my profile (i.e., no "I like walks on the beach, too!")*
>
> *A generic profile devoted to home life, weekends away, wanting a woman who is strong and honest, etc., but which lists no specific hobbies or interests of his own*
>
> *Being widowed (occasionally he will say he is divorced) with a child to care for*
>
> *An epiphany of interest upon seeing my picture ("There is something about you" or "I feel as if we already know one another")*
>
> *His profile picture is way prettier than I am*

---

* No author. "Signs of a Nigerian Dating Scammer." chanceforlove.com. 22 December 2006. Web. 20 May 2011.

The two essential questions to ask are how he handles adverb endings and whether his email could have been copied and pasted twenty times in an hour.

Each time I notified a website of suspected fraud, I received a note telling me the user had been deleted.

Both Danny and Steve had a penchant for bad love clichés in their first emails: "I don't know what else to tell you, but consider this: To laugh is to risk appearing a fool. To weep is to risk appearing sentimental. To reach out for another is to risk involvement. To expose feelings is to risk exposing of yourself." Blah blah blah.

As many scammer-wary websites note, Danny and Steve immediately asked to communicate via Yahoo!, rather than through websites that try, and obviously often fail, to run checks on IP addresses before posting profiles. The more traffic they generate through an offshore IP address, the more likely they'll be found out and blacklisted from a site. It's easier to pull the wool over someone's eyes by going straight to email rather than communicating through the site.

Scammers pick out a specific American burg as their home, but Steve was stupid enough to say that he lived in Carroll Gardens, a neighborhood bordering the Heights. I asked him to meet me for coffee and he didn't know where the Heights's main thoroughfare, Montague Street, was and, anyway, he had been waiting to watch the soccer game that was about to come on. The next day he was headed to Washington on business that would take him to Nigeria. "Oh, not another one," I moaned in response. "I suppose you'll be awarded a large sum of money you'll need my help getting out of the country, too."

"What you talking about, woman?" he screamed back, not knowing his diction was a dead giveaway.

After notifying OkCupid's administrator, I got caught up in researching Internet fraud. I found whole web communities, such as romancescam.com or scamdigger.com, which give you the tools to locate a suspect's IP address and location, upload a photograph to match against other people's experiences, and space not only for war stories but to add to the data on a scammer.

I decided to see what Danny Foster's photo brought up.

A month after I returned the bathroom linens, he had conned a woman who was in the vulnerable position of just having lost a loved one out of a large sum of money. Two photos he'd sent me were posted, as were a number of "Hellie." I was able to add a second email address, another photograph and the name of his "receiver" (who I suspect is one and the same as Danny Foster) in Cotonou.

There is a similar aspect in the stories of victims: Many were especially vulnerable due to a death, divorce, breakup or other crisis. My dealings with Benin Boy began about seven weeks after Dar and I went to Santa Fe. I must not have been truly in love, I thought as I read these women's backstories. It never occurred to me to send money, and my fantasies about the handsome man in the photos didn't evolve.

Maybe I'm smarter than other women.

Or maybe the possibility that I would lose the foundational respect from my best friend was bigger than true love and feline-level curiosity put together.

Thanks for having my back, Betts.

Six

The female cane toad inflates her body to prevent mating, making it difficult for the male toad to get a grip.

Relying on a 2009 survey, eHarmony claims responsibility for "nearly five percent of marriages in America." Their website doesn't say whether this five percent is per year or of all marriages—nor, for that matter, does it define "America."

I was teaching freshman composition that summer and I was righteously anal about such vagaries. But then, the language of love is pretty much entirely corrupt.

Of course I couldn't delete eHarmony's introduction to Eric. A day or two later, I couldn't resist writing. "Well, well, well," I said. "So much for eHarmony's claims to infallible matches." Eric responded that he was doing research for his book on sexual networking and that eHarmony's claim of twenty million registered users is misinformation. Users do not have to be members. Registration is free and anyone becomes part of the pool of matches sent out to users every day. But if you want to *communicate* with one of those matches, you have to fork over between $23.95 and $44.94 a month. I had, in the interests of finding my "soul mate," enrolled for three months, which is why I was able to write Eric. He had no curiosity about what I was doing there. Maybe he read my blogs after all. I occasionally wrote about my adventures and observations for this book.

Getting people to spend money after promises of free membership is true of all websites. Each has its own hook, but the bait is that if you want to do more than nod at someone, one party or the other will have to fish out its MasterCard.

The hook of eHarmony is that after quizzing users on the "29 Dimensions® of Compatibility," each person receives matches that could lead to the Holy Grail: an LTR (long-term relationship) and ultimately asking her fat cousin to read 1 Corinthians while the skinny friends stand on the altar in shiny, unnatural dresses.

Thus I discovered I am primarily a "Negotiator," someone who dislikes both conflict and being crowded by her partner.

So there are some problems with the 29 Dimensions® of Compatibility. The test sounds reassuringly scientific but don't adults have some self-knowledge? Are we looking for compatibility? It's a nice feeling but it's not exactly in the troubadour tradition. A random selection of definitions from various standard dictionaries and thesauruses brings up the following matches for "compatible": harmonious, consistent, able to be used with something, able to cross-pollinate, able to coexist together, able to be friends, open to possibility, in agreement, love (which Microsoft Bookshelf's first definition of is "two hearts that beat as one"), capable of forming a chemically or biochemically stable system, capable of being used in transfusion or grafting, designed to work with another device or system.

Basically, compatibility is terrific stuff for college dorm mates or the rearing of children. But for a dating site, admitting the meaning of compatibility would not sell memberships. The exception—love that is two hearts beating as one—is another concept designed by poets to fuck us up, and eHarmony's success stories speak exactly that age-old jabberwocky of romance.

"It was like meeting somebody I already knew," one eHarmony bride remembers.

"There was instant chemistry," recalls another.

"You get to see inside of the person before you see the person."

"We both realized there had been something larger than either one of us at work that day [we met]."

"I felt as if I was finally home."

"I met my soul mate . . . I'm just so grateful."*

I may be a curmudgeon, but these people are mouthing the words of Hallmark and/or their preachers. I've had that dizzy, arms-open-to-the-night-sky-that-gives-diamonds feeling; I've met a man I think I must have known in another life. Despite being able to finish each other's sentences, we both had a touch of altitude sickness and, maybe (at least on the men's

* eharmony.com. 2011. Web. May 29, 2011.

parts), wanted not to know what the other person was thinking before it got said.

• • •

A big problem with any other dating site's correlate of the 29 Dimensions® of Compatibility* is that these tests rely on an unshifting self-esteem on the part of the hopeful member. When I was at my thinnest and most physically exuberant, I maxed out one of my credit cards on a matchmaking service that is now out of business. I'd profiled my feelings about myself and what I was looking for, made a video and sat back to see the men they'd choose for me. I wouldn't have dated their candidates on the most ego-drained day of my life. Why did I receive these potential dates? Because on the service's scale, *they* thought they were hot.

Similarly, when I signed on for three months of eHarmony (for a whopping $134.85, or six and three-quarters hour-long walks with the most vicious dog on my ex-client roster), I was feeling both good about losing twenty or so pounds and defiant about apologizing for and hiding in my weight. I gave myself honest ratings on body size *and* I gave myself high ratings for being pretty and stylish.

---

* eHarmony defines these categories as "emotional temperament, social style, cognitive mode, physicality, relationship skills, values and beliefs, key experiences."

No one responded.

Of course, the forty-one questions eHarmony asks allow for many other reasons for male silence, and I've never had a great deal of success with dating services that focus narrowly on the mainstream.* The writer-thing is weird, my income inconsistent, my aims in life vague. I hated the Guided Communication multiple-choice ice-breakers for being so narrow and, in general, the matches I received weren't spot-on.

"James" was a typical suggestion. He was tall, had no children, and smoked—enough information for me to look deeper into his profile. The most influential person in his life was John Rothschild, his favorite leisure time activities were playing poker, racing cars, skiing and riding horses. *Atlas Shrugged* was the most important book he ever read.

Dr. Warren? We have a problem.

NASCAR and Ayn Rand are the two items in the world I am most contemptuous of. At fifty-three I was not inclined to take up skiing. I have no idea who John Rothschild is.

He had two other answers that troubled me. He wished more people would notice "the depth of my soul" and one of his best life skills was "using humor to make friends laugh."

Never trust anyone who claims a sense of humor. He will depend on jokes rather than wit and will consider himself to be

---

* It took the threat of a New Jersey anti-discrimination lawsuit in 2009 for eHarmony to open a sister site, Compatible Partners, that serves gay men and lesbians. queerty.com. 31 March 2009. Web. 31 May 2011.

the funny one in the relationship. As for using humor to produce laughter, the composition teacher alarms in my head were deafening.

Never trust anyone who uses the word "soul." He doesn't know what he's talking about and will either be grossly disappointed in his partner or will expect marriage, with a fancy wedding cribbed from the Wedding Network, to last until the day one of them dies and the search for the fairy tale starts again.

. . .

The most popular quest on dating websites is the search for one's soul mate. Hindu theology believes that couples are predetermined in heaven and that the soul, the animating spark or machinery of our minds and bodies, therefore has one mate. In *Symposium*, Plato's study of the nature of love, Aristophanes relates that humans were once two-headed, four-legged and -armed creatures who threatened the gods so much that Zeus split them in two and as a result, humans are always looking for their other half (literally).

I've taken the time to explore the hoo-ha of soul mates that is sold by the marriage-minded dating sites, because it is so widespread. While I believe the statistic is imprecise and self-serving, 2003 polls found that 80 percent of American daters believe they have one person out there for them but wouldn't recognize him or her if they met. "My other half" is a concept that is absurd and, worse, insulting. If I buy into the idea that a boyfriend or lover is "the one person who can always make [me] smile, who shares [my] hopes and dreams, who makes [me] whole,"* then my report card at the pearly gates will be full of Incompletes. No one can induce me to smile all the time. My sanity depends on the evolution of my hopes and dreams. The men who could finish my sentences have left and I've changed a lot of my sentences.

Any intelligent man has to consider that the hoops the marriage-material sites ask him to jump through, the restrictions he is given in looking for date material and the amount of money he has to pay is the measure of his naïveté, desperation and, perversely, his laziness.

And if you can't give up your innocence and lack of wholeness, you can always follow up on one of eHarmony's advertisers and cough up *another* hundred-plus bucks and get books, DVDs or CDs instructing you on how to make "any guy" addicted to you.

． ． ．

And then there's chemistry, that ineffable and yet somewhat measurable "it" that can get us into a world of trouble.

Chemistry is quantifiable in that there are a number of odorless pheromones secreted by the male and female body. Male androstadienone, found in sweat, is one among other biological yanks to the endocrine system that pumps out the hormones that make us women randy but choosy, fertile and experiencing PMS simultaneously.

---

* Blade, Lina. Urbandictionary.com. 14 June 2004. Web. 31 May 2011.

But it is also ineffable in that chemicals are part of the mysterious stuff that has made the human race multiply and thrive. Typically, this means that men look—often unconsciously—for younger, healthy women with symmetrical features and a low hip-to-shoulder ratio,* while women tend to look for older men. Darwin would understand. That ideal woman is most likely to give birth to healthy, attractive children who will go on to propagate the species and the graying man probably has more resources to protect his progeny.

And this is why American women spend more annually on improving our looks than we do on education.†

All of that, however, applies to meeting someone in person. In cyberspace, you can find love at first sight according to whatever way you want—or need—to twist a person's words and looks to suit your own.

Which is how I met Patrick.

    • • •

"I didn't date when I was fat," Bette said. "As soon as I outgrew my size ten jeans, I quit."

It is one of women's hundred-year-old questions: Do we have the right to be romantic when we are fat? For forty years I

---

* http://www.staff.ncl.ac.uk/daniel.nettle/procroysoc.pdf. 10 May 2013.

† Patzer, Gordon. *Looks: Why They Matter More Than You Ever Imagined.* New York: American Management Association. 2008. Kindle edition.

assumed I did not. In my few years of dating in a normal-size body I learned three important things: 1) men wanted or didn't want to sleep with me for all the other stuff behind the size ten Ralph Laurens, 2) there are schmucks to fit any sized woman, and 3) no matter how thin I got, I was still embarrassed by the wreckage of my past obesity.

"You should talk to Pam," Bette advised.

It was a brilliant call. Pam is intrepid. At over 300 pounds, she has at least two boyfriends in addition to her estranged husband, one of them culled from the Internet.

"There are a thousand sites for curvy people," Pam said in her heavy Brooklyn accent. "I met Hal on BBWCupid." She pronounced his name "Hail." I always listen carefully to Pam for overlooked nuances.

"Here's the deal, though," I said. "I've lost about twenty pounds and I want very much to keep on going. How do I say that?"

"Just . . . I dunno," she floundered. "Don't say that dieting is the most important thing in your life." Dating code for weight-watching is embedded in the phrase "exercise daily," but it's still de rigueur to say that you love to cook and eat out, even if it's a lettuce leaf and a glass of club soda. Not even income is as coy in doublespeak as what men and women do for their calories. "I guess play it cool. Don't mention it."

Like my smoking. I answer yes on the questionnaires if my choices are simply yes or no, but am relieved when one of the options is "trying to quit," and I never smoke on a first date unless he does, too.

"Keep me posted! This is exciting!"

Pam was wrong about the thousand sites for corpulent humans. There were about twenty when I Googled fat/chubby/large dating. I chose the two links that came up most often and went to work on my profile.

I called Pam back. "So what do you think of this? 'The words "Let's pretend" still transport you immediately.'"

"That's a *goood* one," she cooed.

"Thanks," I said. "It ends, 'This doesn't have to be difficult. Only impossible.'"

I heard the intake of Pam's cigarette. "It sounds beautiful," she said. Doubt dripped from her voice. "Definitely . . . arty."

"I'm arty," I said. "Maybe my standards are that guys understand or intuit what I'm saying here."

"M'm." I could see the smoke ring hovering in the thick air of a July afternoon in Park Slope. "Lemme know as soon as you hear from someone."

She was no longer speaking in exclamation points.

But I am arty, I argued to myself. *I do want a guy to get what I'm saying out of sympathy rather than a dictionary.*

I clicked "post."

· · ·

"*Great* hair" was the subject line of the email from "PatrickBigHeart" on Venus Diva Dating ("for Curvy Romance"). "Do you still wear it in a bob?" I flashed back to the shoe freak and wannabe slave of craigslist, but then he added, "I could get lost in a smile like that and I'm a huge fan of John LeCarry, too."

I sat back and folded my arms. Aside from his misspelling of the best espionage writer ever (was he spelling it phonetically or am I the only one addicted to Google and inserting accents in my prose?), I'd described my ideal man as being a combination of a pirate and George Smiley. This could be interesting.

His profile described him as fifty-five, two inches taller than I, and divorced with a couple of kids living on their own. His picture showed he was in possession of a full head of gray hair, with smile lines grooving parentheses from his eyes to his chin.

Beyond flattering me, his email added that he lived in Bay Ridge and was in public relations at one of the big magazine consortiums.

I could have purred.

·   ·   ·

"Why is someone as cute as you on Big Fat Divas?" I asked when he called after an exchange of emails. Neither of us believed in long written correspondence.

He laughed. "I like women with some curves."

I've never gotten that. Fat women have some protrusions but are as devoid of curves as Kate Moss.

"Curves like Mitzi Gaynor?"

"Nooo. Curves like yours. So, Frances, you like to play pretend. What do you pretend?"

It was after nine. I was done teaching for the week, had no papers to mark and was freshly showered and wearing my favorite nightie. Daisy was sleeping with her head on my foot. Patrick liked big women. Life was good.

"Well," I drawled, "right now I'm pretending we're past all the awkward stuff and wondering what we do on a Saturday night when the heat is this ghastly."

He sighed the New York sigh of so-many-things-to-do/ so-little-I-really-want-to-do. New Yorkers become blasé at some point in midlife. Only the culture vultures with subscriptions and favorite prima ballerinas are not put off by late-night subways after the age of fifty. "I'd take you to my favorite restaurant and I'd make sure the air conditioner was on full blast," Patrick said. "Do you like Southern cooking?"

· · ·

The air of Ninth Avenue was thick with exhaust fumes and the smell of garlic and seafood as I waited for Patrick in the green and violet dusk. Except for the heat creating pockets of discomfort along my back and thighs, I would have felt quite fetching in my new favorite dress, which would best be described as Lucy Ricardo stuck at Petticoat Junction with the Honeymooners. After the walk from Times Square, the scratchy crinoline was starting to feel limp.

How, I wondered, does Pam stay fresh and unmussed for her BigFatFolksDotCom dates?* Had Bette been smart to with-

---

* She drives everywhere, I remembered.

draw from the Dating Wars when she crossed the threshold of sweat pooling in back fat? Maybe she was right. As soon as she gave up, Johnny, the owner of a local pizzeria who'd always stopped everything to exchange raunchy remarks with her, hounded her into a date and, three months and another sixty pounds later, marriage. They argue over everything from their mothers to the Cyclones' batting averages, and have his-and-hers fish tanks: blue angels for Johnny, a lone piranha for Bette.

Between jealousy of cars and fish, I wondered why I hadn't chosen a pocketbook that would have held a book.

By the time I reminded myself that at least I'd worn comfortable flats and hadn't put on mascara on this 85-degree night, a man in jeans and a pink polo shirt, carrying a book bag with—oh, my—dragons on it sauntered up and kissed me on the cheek.

"Sorry I'm late. I wanted to pick something up for you. Let's go in."

I don't believe I've ever been to a restaurant that has a roll of paper towels on each table, and I've had barbecue in dive spots in the Georgia Appalachians and Louisiana bayou country.

But it was nearly cold inside, and the varnished wood of the booth felt glorious against my sticky back.

Patrick flashed the waitress that grin I'd fallen for on Venus Diva and ordered something I didn't catch. I hoped it was cold and wet.

He pulled a purple foil bag out and put it reverently on the table. Godiva dark chocolate truffles. "I've been thinking about you eating these," he said, and smiled again. "'Course, you might want to wait until . . . later."

Was that creepy? I thanked him and wished I'd thought to bring an offering.

The waitress came back and set down big glasses of iced tea. Sugary iced tea. I wasn't doing sugar at the time. I set it down as the waitress's perfect ass disappeared toward the kitchen and pulled my water glass closer. Patrick had disappeared in the menu, which was so big that when I opened mine, we could have camped out in them.

"If we get the combo we'll get a little of everything. The sweet potato fries are great."

"Wow," I said, looking at the promise of more meat than Ted Turner's ranch. I craned over the side of my menu to see what other people had. The answer seemed to be, a lot.

"The pulled chicken is also great," Patrick's voice flumed up from the bowels of the menu. "You really can't go wrong here."

Our waitress was back with plates of fried things. "Have you decided what you'd like for dinner?" she asked.

I began to open my mouth but Patrick flirted up at her. "What do you recommend?"

"If you're new here, it's a good idea to go for the Over the Top," she said. He nodded, still studying the entrées. "Okay, let's do that. Aaaannnd let's do the mac-and-cheese, too. With bacon."

What's four months of weighing and measuring your food and abstaining from sugar and flour when you have a plate of fried green tomatoes in front of you and the promise of onion rings on the way? I butted in as he debated sides and asked for collard greens. It was probably the healthiest thing on the menu if you couldn't manage to request a salad.

"Try these," Patrick said, and put an egg roll on my plate. I cut it open and cheese and chopped beef spilled out. Philly cheesesteak in pastry.

"Wow," I said again.

∙ ∙ ∙

"Have you dated a lot on Big Fat Divas?" I asked as I salted a tomato.

"As often as I've found a woman of real substance," he said. "There aren't that many from New York and not that many who are smart and funny on top."

Yes, that's about right, I thought. *I'm all on top, smart, funny, nice smile and hair: the dateable head.*

"What are the women like?"

"Warm-hearted, enjoy family time and good conversation."

"Just like the men, then."

"Probably."

"Do you glaze over when you read profiles?" I asked. "I do. I end up looking at the middle of the paragraph and if there's something there, then I might back up."

"That's why I wrote you as soon as I saw your ad. I was impressed you had a full-body photo. And you made me laugh. My only hesitation was your choice of dining and the fact that you're on a diet."

"Yeah, well, I could stand to lose . . . a lot."

"The women on that site are pretty much okay with their bodies."

"I wanted to be honest."

"But you look great."

Our waitress was back with an enormous tray of cholesterol. I sat back and listened to Patrick *ooh* over each platter she set down. I hoped they had doggie bags. Daisy was going to love Patrick.

I helped myself to a piece of chicken and a couple of sweet potato fries as Patrick sliced off a couple of ribs.

"Thank you for the compliment," I said.

"No, thank you for coming," he said, and toasted me with his iced tea and one foot nudging mine under the table. "It's really amazing, seeing you . . . like this."

I looked at the heaps of food between us. Neither of us had touched the coleslaw or the macaroni and cheese in its nifty skillet. I looked down at my chest and dabbed my mouth, then allowed a few syllables of laughter.

"What? At night? In public? Eating without getting barbecue sauce in my hair?"

"No, no. But that could be kind of . . . sexy."

. . .

We divided the meat up between us to take home and left the rest, which included carnage from the deep-fried Twinkies with strawberries that we'd shared. Getting to the subway shouldn't have been a problem. I could just roll there.

Patrick offered to drop me home by cab.

. . .

I was angry with myself. The piers of Twelfth Avenue fell behind us and we sped through the swank romance of the Meatpacking District. Good route home, I thought. I am definitely packed.

I was angry with Patrick for talking so much about not dieting and not leaving me room even to order my own drink.

I was stuffed and hot and thirsty. I wanted to walk Daisy and then languish in a cool bath. When I could breathe a little, I wanted cold cold water.

"I won't come in, if you don't mind," Patrick said as we climbed onto the Brooklyn Bridge. I love that crossing at night: the string of jade beads of the Verrazano and the blaze of jade of the Statue of Liberty. It was muggy, though, and the green distance was smudged with haze.

"Not a problem," I said. "I wasn't expecting company and I'm pretty tired after all that food."

"I'll call you when I get home," he added, and squeezed my hand. I felt like Twinkie cream and barbecue sauce were going to ooze from the joints of my fingers.

. . .

"He's cute!" I told Daisy, doling out the after-walkies Milk-Bone and scutching my sandals off. I pulled off my shruggie and dropped it on a dresser I pretended was immune from dog hair. "Very nice. *Very* generous. But weird, you know? The kind of guy you would bark and lunge at." I peeled myself out of the rest of my clothes and began running a tepid bath with Dead Sea salts. I needed to be leached.

The phone rang as I was wandering around pinning up my hair as the tub filled. Without thinking I picked up.

"Hey," Patrick breathed. "How're you doing?"

"Hot," I answered. "I'm running a bath."

"R'rrr," he growled.

"Trust me, I'm way too lazy to be one of those women with the sixty-two votive candles and *Bolero* on the CD player."

"Still," he said. "I'd—"

"Daisy!" I shouted at my flopped and innocent dog. When I told him I wasn't up for company, I meant it, and I was ready to yell at my dog to get my way. There was something off about this guy. Remember, this observation was coming from the girl who believes in wait-and-see when it comes to boys who like her first. "Ugh," I said. "I gotta go pick up the trash she just knocked over. Email me. Okay, babe?"

"Check it when you get out of the bath."

. . .

A summit conference was in order. It was three big girls who sat down at Starbucks the next evening: Bette, small, wide, with skin that reminds me of Italian plums; Pam, tall, blonde and built like a brick house; me, a little thinner than either, dark hair and pale-skinned, still wearing the semi-professional clothes from teaching that afternoon.

"So he's cute as Hello Kitty," I tell them. "But he'd only talk about restaurants and food and how much he likes taking women out to eat and how pretty he thinks I am. And don't say, 'Well, you are,' because he said it too often for someone who wasn't starry-eyed crazy-in-love."

"Okay," Pam said, stirring her thousand-ingredient macchiato-thingy. "He sounds nice, though."

"But hang on, 'cause I'm sitting there thinking he works for this huge magazine company. He must have gossip about models and editors and manufacturers. He'd commented how much he likes John le Carré. And all we're doing is trading favorite entrées. And I think, well, at least we're talking. I mean, how many first dates have you guys been on where the silence is like a wall?" Bette and Pam groaned. "He wouldn't let me tip for dinner or the cab. How many first dates have you guys been on where the guy actually paid?"

"I wouldn't let a guy pay for a first date," Bette said. "It's cleaner. You're your own woman."

"I think it's gentlemanly," Pam said. She's near sixty and had to wear bloomers in high school gym. "I don't expect it, but I like it."

"Hang on," I cut in. "It gets weird. He makes some noise about not coming over to my house, as though I had invited him, and then when I can't talk when I get home he emails that he's going to fall asleep thinking of me naked, eating these chocolates he gave me, that he wants to—"

"Don't!" Bette nearly shrieked. "This is gonna be disgusting, isn't it?"

"Yup. Short and sweet? He likes to fuck women while they

eat. Dinner's like foreplay. I lost my damn abstinence* because I didn't know how to say no."

"We've all done it," Pam said sympathetically.

"Usually after the date, though," Bette added. "This guy, Patrick? He sounds like one of those weirdos." She starts snapping her fingers. "Feeders. That's it. I thought they were, like, obese hummingbirds when I first heard of them."

"Jee-*zus*. Of course."

"What?" Pam demanded.

"They're people who get off on watching fat people gorge themselves and getting fatter."

"*Ho*ly Jesus," Pam said.

"Drop him, Frances, and drop the subject," Bette spat. "It's too horrendous."

"Although," Pam added, "if they get off on seeing you get bigger, they at least have to stick around . . ." She looked at us, but Bette was sitting at a right angle to the table and I still couldn't get my jaw to close. "I'm just saying. I'd like a guy to hang around awhile, you know?"

* * *

I went home and did some research on Feederism, a fetish that the National Association to Advance Fat Acceptance condemns for its adverse health consequences. There is a whole spectrum

---

* "Abstinence" is the phrase for the 12-step food plan I follow.

of sexual practices involving pretending to be fatter or getting fatter, whether it's through calories, costumes or a reservation for an orgy of animal fat.

And, like every other subgroup, there are dating websites just for feeders and feedees. I emailed the links to Patrick, along with my gracious thanks for the deep-fried Twinkies.

I'd always thought *9 1/2 Weeks* was stupid but at least I understood why it continued to sell.

Seven

Each breeding season, male humpback whales sing a new tune, which might incorporate bits of last season's melodies or be new releases. These new songs pass from whale to whale for four thousand miles.

Any chronicler of dating is presented with a challenge in that good dates are generally alike. It is unhappy dating that, as Tolstoy says of families, is unique in its unhappiness and therefore lends itself to storytelling. So far, I'd been courted by jerks, freaks, fundamentalists and criminals, but my luck was about to run out. I would come to look back on my early summer's abortive tries with nostalgia. Not only were they excellent practitioners of their weirdness, but they had no desire to pit their weirdness against mine.

Using a date to play *Jeopardy!* is exhausting.

. . .

One morning, after I had harvested my crops and collected rents on my Facebook games, thereby keeping up my position in the higher ranks of my Farm and City friends, I found myself looking for more ways to put off marking forty essays. I decided to weed out my email accounts and landed at my dating inbox. There wasn't time to troll through all the exciting news (!) each site had to offer about tips, hot dates, special deals, psychological insights and the latest success stories, so I deleted steadily until I got to "You have a new message."

The first paper on my pile was about gangsta rap.

I opened the message with a micro-prayer that it would make me forget that the second essay was on the controversy over the balls used in the World Cup.

"Looking for Lou" was—har-har—named Lou, DWM, no children. He wrote that he was a junior high math teacher and had just spent a month bicycling around Ireland. He picked up on my statement that my hobbies include what I call "travel porn." "I definitely need to know more about that!"

I quickly typed a note about my compulsion to plan trips to places on my bucket list, even though I had neither money nor time to take them. I sent it, sighed and went back to essays.

By the time I worked my way through a scramble of verb tenses, Lou wrote back that he was boning up on elliptic functions for a summer course he was taking and finishing off a cold key lime soufflé from a dinner party he'd had the night before; did I want to have dinner in the Heights that evening?

* * *

Lou was so tall and skinny that he made me think of Ichabod Crane. I laughed as I waited for the light to change, and I watched his smile widen. He didn't know that I was thinking that, at five foot eight, I'm used to wearing flats on first dates. I could have worn stilts that night.

My tummy fluppered. Why does one person respond to another? Was it because I'd Googled elliptic functions and found a quote from a nineteenth-century mathematician, "Invert, always invert"? and it had reminded me of E. M. Forster's "Connect, only connect"? Had I pre-primed myself or was I smitten because his worn jeans hung from his hips and he wore a faded Good-bye Kitty T-shirt?

Is it ironic that I like skinny men, or is it some kind of Freudian Cupid Complex in which I am doomed to seek Otherness? Or, in this case, was it that my blind, ninety-three-year-old father, who I adore, had finished a lecture series on algebra that spring? Was it my Electra complex tricking me into a sudden surge of hope against the odds of a second date from a guy whose eyes were bluer than his picture showed?

I kissed Lou hello and he took my elbow to hurry me into the restaurant, muttering, "Great, great" to himself. Was that a nervous or a sarcastic reaction to this business of showing up on time with clean hair and a smiling welcome? I wasn't sure I liked being hurried inside so quickly.

And thus it was. From the startlement of sky blue eyes to being herded was a fast fall.

"I eat a lot of salad," I warned him as we looked over the menu. "And a lot of chicken. There's a chance I'll wake up one morning sprouting feathers."

Lou nodded thoughtfully. "I try to eat as many raw vegetables as possible, myself. And I actually like tofu." He looked at me directly for a second or two. "Do you like tofu?"

"To play jacks with," I said. To his blank stare I mimed bouncing a ball and scooping up markers. Nothing. I shook my head but smiled as brightly as I could. "Maybe boys didn't play jacks. You need a small rubber ball that bounces well. The tofu—"

"—is rubbery," he cut in. "You need to experiment with it. I make a great lemon pepper dish with it."

Tofu

Lou: 1

Frances: 0

I squared my shoulders and decided to order the chef salad with its glories of cheese, ham and salami. A small voice in my head sneered, "Yeah, but an American of our age should have got the jacks joke." I slapped the menu shut and asked for blue cheese dressing on the side.

He ordered the salmon Caesar salad.

I could have predicted that.

*　*　*

"Did you love Ireland?" I asked. "I've never been but want to go so badly."

Lou sat back and fiddled with his cutlery. "It was . . . life-changing. I got off the plane in Shannon with a backpack and my folding bicycle and jet lag. I had a rough itinerary and a couple of reservations. It was wild. I made it as far as Coonagh that morning before I had to stop and crash for the day. It was like biking on acid or something. The sun was out, everything looked like it was supposed to, but there was this gloss on it . . . or the edges were softened. Something. The whole trip was like that. Much slower than I thought because I had to really *look* to see the edges and angles."

Our salads arrived and I sighed with pleasure, at what he was saying and at the prospect of food. "It sounds amazing."

"Yes . . ."

"No, I mean, literally amazing. Jaw-dropping-in-the-moment-awareness-amazing."

He looked at me a moment, then chopped a piece of romaine into a bite-size piece. "Exactly. That's it. Tell me about this travel porn you mentioned on Senior People Meet."

"I plan trips. I look up a place I might want to go and read up on it. Then I order the Dorling Kindersley guide and look at tour guides on YouTube. I can't take the trips, of course. Or only, like, point-oh-oh-one percent of them. Right now I'm saving to go to Amsterdam and Brussels during tulip time. I hope next year." I sighed. "I used to have a lot of freedom and not much money. Now I'm teaching and have neither."

"Amsterdam is amazing," he said. "The Tropenmuseum—"

I cut him off with a fanfare of turkey strip. Whenever I talked about going some place on the usual American Express tours, people seemed to think I needed help. "I was there when I was an undergraduate. Have you ever been to Keukenhof?" The bulb gardens were my ace in the hole because fewer people go to Holland in April. "I like to take pictures," I added.

"Oo-hh." He sounded knowing. He had slotted me as One

of Those: the folks who have to have pictures to prove they went somewhere.

I chewed my turkey and watched him with narrowed eyes. "You probably didn't take a camera to Ireland, did you?"

"Uh, no, actually—"

"Pity. I'd love to have seen pictures. I actually sold a photo I took in Prague last fall. From my Flickr album, if you can believe it." My voice was gay and I was smiling as I said this. His eyes darted across my face and onto the prints on the wall behind me. "I don't know how to use my camera very well but I'll bet you'd conquer one in a heartbeat. It's more left brain than I own."

We busied ourselves with our salads at that. There was malice behind my words, but I liked this Lou-guy. I liked the idea of this tall man brazening out Ireland on a collapsible bicycle with the rain and sun and whatever sound track he lived by as companions. *Please*, I pleaded with him as we ate. *Don't make assumptions about me and don't tell me what to do in Amsterdam.*

"How did your trip change your life?" I asked.

"I was free. I'd go days without talking except to buy food or to get directions. I decided somewhere in Galway that I want to live that way. I have twenty-seven years in with the public schools. I'll go to twenty-eight and retire."

"And do what?" I asked. I envisioned him on a bike in Norway in June and on a bike in Australia in January.

"I'm on this date." He laughed. "It's been a long time since I've been on a date. So that's the first thing. I'd like to take more classes in advanced mathematical theory, complex variables and stuff. I've been volunteering at the Madison community garden and I'm playing electric guitar in a band. We're doing covers of oldies."

I groaned to myself. I hate doo-wop.

"You know—Harold Arlen, Glenn Miller. Those guys."

My heart leapt. That's how I grew up, drinking that music with my baby formula as my parents put on their stiff, whispering evening wear for a night of dancing.

The scalding non-conversation about music with Dar was recent. At least I had a chance in this one.

"That's fantastic!" I said, visions of being called forward, a new Annie Hall, charming if tending to go off-key in the blue light of "Seems Like Old Times."

"We're doing an anniversary party in September, maybe some club dates in bars. I came back from Ireland wanting to live out loud, I guess."

I didn't know what to make of this budding John Pizzarelli. He'd scored on tofu but I tied him with photography, he was winning my heart (or whatever it is when you're still splitting the bill) with Glenn Miller, only to leave the door wide open on "live out loud," which is what the Oxygen Channel commands its mostly female viewers to do during the Saturday night primetime Jennifer Aniston movie when about the only things you do out loud are cry (at spending Saturday night with Aniston) and scrape (ice cream spoon against dish, the last edible puff of popcorn). Nothing makes me feel like more of a spinster than hearing that motto coming out of my TV.

So I smiled and suggested we walk down to the Promenade.

Romantic matters tend to be decided on the Promenade at night. If push has a good chance of coming to shove, it's going to happen with the panoply of downtown Manhattan painted across the river and sky.

"Do you have a favorite song?" Lou asked as we walked down Montague.

"That's an impossible question," I answered. "It depends on my mood and the circumstances and every other thing I can think of."

"Okay, composer."

"H'mm. Bach. But if you're asking because of your band, I'd go with Gershwin."

"Not bad," he said. "How about Kern?" He began humming a slow, sad tune and dwindled into a few words, " 'Yesterdays . . . Days I knew . . . ' Know that song?"

"Nope," I said, and kept walking as I stared straight ahead.

He started again with a soft little scat and then, "Keep on smilin'." He looked down at me.

"Nope," I said again.

He sighed heavily. Was he one up on music in general or two up on individual songs? Where's Alex Trebek when I need him? I considered singing Will's "We dined on garr-bage" song. It never failed to have me in stitches, but I didn't think Lou was interested in getting a laugh out of his music.

Ironic, then, that he turned jaunty and jivey and I let him go on before cutting in with *Den mann Mackie Messer nennt.* I laughed. "That was too easy," I chided. "I have the original cast recording of *Threepenny Opera*. Berlin, 1930: can you imagine? What was Hitler doing in 1930?"

He laughed, too. "Mackie Messer, huh?"

We walked along the iron railing over the skeletons of the old waterfront being turned into one of those parks every Iron Belt city has these days. I hate competition. It makes me shrink and feel stupid. I looked up at him as I sang, "You say knife and I say *Messer*, you say chest, I say dresser. Knife, *Messer*, chest, dresser. Let's call the whole thing off."

"So you do know something about the era."

"Uh, yeah. Bits and pieces. Sometimes I surprise myself and know the lyrics and then again I'll think I know them and can only get through a line or two."

"You have a nice voice," he said.

"Thank you. It helps when I get to choose the register." As compliments go, that's got to be my favorite—and least received.

He walked me home and kissed me on the lips, chastely.

"I enjoyed the evening," I said.

"Me, too. Let's do it again sometime."

"I look forward to it."

He turned and walked back toward the R train. I told Daisy that I liked this one, I thought, that maybe that I'd misinterpreted, and he wasn't trying to one-up me. If I was lucky, I'd impressed him as someone who has her own Stuff. A traveler, a taker of pictures, not so thoroughly dumb about music. Witty, I hoped. Daisy snuffled along the gutters looking for chicken bones and Cheerios and had no advice on the subject. She pretty much loves any visitor and lives for sleepovers when she can slither in between two sets of adoring hands.

With that in mind, I wrote him a quick email, thanking him for the stories and telling him his journey interested me. Had he used the word "journey" with me I would have choked but it's the sort of word most people love thinking they are a part of.

I waited three days before deleting his email address. I remembered after I did so that he'd been singing "Wives and Lovers" under his breath when we walked home. I should have taken that ("There are girls at the office, and men will be men . . .") as a warning.

While I was at it, I should have listened to my own warning in the half-conscious sound track of "But Not for Me" that had been playing in my own head.

* * *

I was already laughing when I sat down at the bar to wait for Galean. A friendly Goth girl in polka dots and crinolines brought me a club soda and laughed back when I said, "I'm meeting a guy for the first time and it doesn't matter what he's like. *This* is a date!"

It was also *my* date. I'd posted it on How About We, a New York–centric site on which people propose specific dates. How About We is romantic, but it also has a huge spirit of fun that leaves room for kindred desires that might not include sex. I'd read about it in the *Times*, which tracked dating trends through its postings. In June, it seemed, everyone was eating fish tacos.

The one time I had gone bowling it was fun. I was bad at it but there's an element of luck in it, too. So I suggested bowling and found myself at Bowlmor Lanes on University Place. It's decorated by someone whose own dating profiles would highlight his favorite movies as *Blade Runner* and *The Wizard of Oz*, and who chose his color palette from the *Smurfs* and Legoland, assisted by Pee-wee Herman. Even if Galean turned out to be Sol from Bleecker Street, my club soda under the déjà vu of all the gay clubs I've been in would be worth it.

An arm reached around me and turned my book over. "*The Beauty Myth*," Galean—at least I supposed it was Galean: he looked like his photo, shaved head, Mephisthophelean beard—said. "Looks heavy." He bopped around a little and took a sip of my drink. "Oh no, Frances. No, no, no. What do you *really* want to drink?"

I looked around and laughed. "Margarita, don't you think?"

"Think? I think it's as much a rule as wearing bowling shoes."

"Although I think a blue Hawaiian would go with the décor better."

"'Anything that you say, I hear myself agree,'" he sang along to the music and hopped up on the stool next to me. "But I think we only want drinks that come decorated with limes. Don't you?"

Galean was thirty years old and cute. I'd recently done the cut-color-eyebrow-treatment rounds at my salon and was wearing a white cotton sweater and a white skirt with a big black belt over black leggings. I felt almost cute enough to be with this kid who had melted into the beat and the vibe without hesitation.

Galean was as delighted by his bowling shoes (red and navy) as I was by mine (green and maroon, like ribbon candy). He hesitated over the balls because they gave him the choice of cherry bombs or watermelons. He bragged that he'd knock down the far left pins, then blamed the Blondie song for destroying his concentration or did a chicken dance in victory. Putting his hand on my shoulder, he gave me wretched advice in a low coach's voice.

He reminded me of Dar. At least until I finished the first margarita. After the second margarita I probably couldn't have told you Dar's last name. By the time we'd bowled four games and drunk three margaritas, I proposed marriage to the mozzarella sticks. We sat on a banquette and drank a last margarita, refusing to give up our shoes until we had to.

"I like the Bingo Players," he said into my ear, "but not for a bowling alley. People waiting their turn or walking up to the lane, they want to sing along."

"Yeah, you were jammin' on Joan Jett out there."

"That's because I *am* Joan Jett." I looked at him skeptically. "Really. My hair is black, I have black eyes, I own a leather jacket."

"You've convinced me," I assure him.

"Bowling should be balletic. Especially when you're as bad as we are. All we can do is work on presentation. Being that I'm Joan Jett, no one had the balls to look at my score. I rule Bowlmor."

"No such luck for me," I lamented. "I can only say that I throw a beautiful gutter."

"Oh, but it's important to throw gutter balls. It's Rosie the Robot's job to retrieve them." He made two high squeaks. I looked at him blankly, then squeaked back in my Flipper voice. "Don't change mediums on me here. I can't make you laugh under water. Let's stay in Orbit City, daughter Judy, and worry about Spacely's Space Sprockets. Understood?"

Maybe it was four margaritas or my string of God-awful dates, or maybe mirth is a dearly loved and dearly missed commodity in my life, but I was rubbing my aching cheeks.

"Because if it wasn't for Spacely's Space Sprockets I'd have to worry I'd drunk to excess and that would defeat George Jetson's computer, which is very specifically against cruelty to humans. Let's give our shoes back and take a walk."

I was surprised to find a bouncer and a velvet rope outside. I don't think Bowlmor discriminates according to looks and connections, but latecomers definitely had to wait their turn while Galean picked out a pink ball and sang, "I hate myself for loving you" to it before rattling it into two pins.

I felt . . . young. The line of pretty people *we* had usurped was a grandeur I couldn't have predicted. It was warm but not as oppressive as four hours ago. NYU students and faux-hipsters filled the sidewalk bars.

"I'm glad I answered your proposal," Galean said. "Most of the dates are pretty pathetic. 'How About We . . . walk the High Line!' It's ninetyfuckingdegrees outside. How About We take a tour of a crematorium!"

"Thank God the bowling alley had air-conditioning made by NASA," I agreed. "What do you usually do on a first date?"

"You're my first date-date since I got divorced," he said.

I stopped. "Wait. You're thirty. You went to college. How much bad stuff can happen in a couple of years? And if I'm a date-date, what did you do on your date?"

"Went out with my best friend and her husband and her best friend. Drank a lot. Went home with the best friend. Now I'm fighting with both my best friend and her best friend."

"Ouch."

"Yeah. The only good thing I can say about her best friend is that she can hold her booze. I have two requirements about women and the first is that they don't go slobbery-stupid when they drink." He kissed me. "You've met this first requirement." He kissed me again.

He was a great kisser.

"You're a great kisser," he said.

"Uhmww," I said as I kissed him.

"Why dontcha take it inside?" someone yelled, and we laughed, rubbing noses before starting to amble down Thirteenth Street.

It is two long blocks to Seventh Avenue and we made it longer. We necked, made out, snogged, pashed. We rouler-ed un patin.* When we got to the subway station I announced I was taking a cab home. I gave him my phone number and told him to call me when he got home to Locust Manor in the far

---

* In French slang, a French kiss is a *patin*, an ice-skating boot. The verb for French kissing means to roll a skate. It kinda makes sense. I guess.

reaches of Queens. Galean hadn't wanted any preliminary chitchat and I thought him a genius for that now.

He snapped his cell phone shut and hailed me a cab, then stopped the next one for his own long trip to Queens. It was after one, far later than I'm used to being out. By two, we'd both come to orgasm and fallen asleep on the phone.

· · ·

If the seeming possibilities of that night were true, tonight his best friend, her husband and her best friend would be noshing on guacamole while I whirred up a batch of something from a nice Puerto Rican rum that Galean and I bought on a visit to his grandmother.

· · ·

I woke, late and hungover, because the phone rang. Galean offered to come to Brooklyn for brunch. I had stacks of essays, which meant I'd given up the niceties of scrubbing the bathroom and dusting. I could give him a clean toilet and bathroom sink and a clean me in the hour and a half before he arrived. When he called from the Clark Street station Daisy and I set out to meet him halfway.

"Who's that?" I asked enthusiastically. I half-crouched and pointed. "Who's that man? Who is it? Is that Uncle Galean?"

This is our routine whenever we see a friend or, today, a new friend. Her tail turns into a blur of anticipation and her ears go back against her head as she shakes and barks. As soon as I'm absolutely sure she has her target I let go of her leash and she runs in her own half-crouch of submissive love. Her lovers will pat their chests so that she jumps up to kiss. Her true lovers will swat her neck and forequarters in play so that she dances a quadrangle through their legs. For her worshippers, she throws herself on her back and gazes knowingly up for a belly rub.

Galean looked askance.

Daisy looked equally askance. She expects that anyone called uncle or auntie will do something. I clapped my hands and she raced back to me.

"This is Daisy," I said.

"I figured. Cute dog. Big."

"I thought I'd introduce you before we go out. Are you hungover or are you hungry?"

"I'm starving. I'm hardly ever hungover. Are you?"

"Very hungry and very hungover. Twenty years ago I could have drunk you under the table but these days I go months without a drink." I stopped to take Daisy inside, then took Galean's arm to guide him toward the pig binge at the Irish bar on Montague. Sausage *and* bacon. Two kinds of pudding. Eggs and home fries and a free Bloody Mary.

The perfect hangover antidote.

And it has booths, a jukebox and, to Galean's amusement, "eggs Benedictine."

I realized he was the first Catholic boy I'd been out with that summer. My heart smiled.

We ordered and then he dragged me to my feet. "Now comes

the important part." He pulled out a five-dollar bill and studied the jukebox as though it was the LSATs. "We want to introduce Sunday gently," he said, and punched in some numbers. "Owl City to start. Then"—he flipped through the stiff pages—"we'll take it up a notch. Ah! Perfect. Now we ratchet it up again but we keep it familiar so that people don't complain about the noise. Good box. They have Amy Winehouse." He flipped some more. "Ian Dury—and it's 'Lullaby for Francis'! How beautiful is that? Yeah, my boy Ian will bring us down to the Jason Mraz and we'll finish with"—the pages clicked to the end and he thwacked the entire catalogue back to the beginning—"Yes. Beta Band. It's feel good, it's mellow as cream in your coffee and people will be wondering where they heard it before." He turned and handed me a fiver. "Your turn."

I've never fancied myself a DJ and know nothing about music anymore. The bands he'd talked about could have been a Chinese dialect. I began turning the pages. I picked "Norwegian Wood," then Annie Lennox giving up on love. Cyndi Lauper's "I Drove All Night." He'd said something about pumping up the beat so I punched in the B-52s and then I was stumped, racking my brain as I clacked from page to page for songs that I liked—and that Galean might like.

"Break on Through" must have been included for last call when the local stud traders and lawyers were drunk enough to fancy themselves their black sheep uncles who were *at* Woodstock, man.

But it's also an important song to me. I play it when I get stuck writing. It helps me punch through the walls of my self. Would Galean get it?

"A jukebox is a test," he said as we tucked in to our pig feast. "I can tell everything about a woman by what she picks."

Oh. F-uuuu-ckkkk. Again with "Rhythm and Blues for a thousand, Alex."

What had I told him? That I'm essentially stuck in the early 1980s. That I'm pretty girlie, what with all that yearning and desperation to escape. I mean, break on through, get out of that state, I drove all night to get to you, set this spirit free, when I awoke I was alone?

Yikes.

His only comment, however, was that he wouldn't have chosen The Doors, "not for a Sunday afternoon." I told him why I like the song as we walked home but he was an aesthete rather than a memoirist.

With a shudder of fear, I realized that only the Orange Rose Guy had been inside my apartment since I'd started this enterprise. The most perspicacious comment anyone has ever made about the Bat Cave is that you should never set anything down because you'll never find it again. Bette is the one person who truly loves the Bat Cave. She sits on my love seat with Daisy attached to her side and looks around, awestruck. "It's like a museum in here, Franny. And it always smells like coffee."

Most people either say "Wow" or something nice but filled with ellipses.

Galean was a Wow.

I didn't want to go to bed with him but I badly wanted to fool around. I suggested we watch a movie and told him to pick something out while I walked Daisy. He handed me the DVD for *Closer* when we got back. I looked around at my lack of seating. The love seat isn't comfortable for two, and my futon was folded over on the floor.

"This is going to sound weird," I said, "but the most comfortable and the cleanest way to watch a movie is make up the futon and for both of to take off clothes we don't want covered in dog hair." He wrinkled his eyebrows. "It's July," I explained. "She's shedding a small poodle every day. And Daisy sleeps with me, so . . ."

He nodded and started taking off his shirt and pants, which I hung up in the bathroom where they were most likely to be out of hair's way.

"This is a come-on," I told him as I unfolded the futon, "but it's a practical come-on."

Daisy was thrilled and plonked herself down between us and pushed her nose into Galean's cheek before turning over for a four-handed belly rub.

I love the feeling of Daisy against my bare skin. Labs are smooth, silky dogs, not dry fluff or curly like, say, a golden retriever or poodle. To me it's the difference between satin and gunnysack and I never get tired of the weight of a dog stretched along my side.

Galean wiped his face and patted her awkwardly. "Nice doggie."

"No, no, no," I said. "This is a Labrador, not some dumb Chihuahua that you can break. *This* is how you pet a Lab." I sat up and took a bulging handful of neck and rubbed her with my knuckles. "You don't pet a Lab. You rearrange them."

At the repositioning of her coat, Daisy turned and flirted up at me. I sang, "Oh come let us adore me, I'm Daisy the dawg" to the tune of "Come All Ye Faithful." Galean laughed anemically.

If July makes her shed, it also reduces her snuggle time. After ten minutes she went off to the cool tiles in the bathroom. Galean quickly closed the gap.

I was impressed by his choice of movie and by how much of his girliness he was in touch with. *Closer* is a thinking person's film, an exploration of multiple attractions and the limpidity of half-realized love. We laughed when Clive Owens spat at Jude Law, "You—you *writer*!" But it's also a very claustrophobic movie, mostly interiors, and some dark ones at that. Doing the hanky-panky helped but by the credits, the Bat Cave looked tawdry and smaller than ever. The light I could sense beyond my windows was thickening and I was exhausted. I told Galean that Daisy and I would walk him to the train.

"I have to tell you something," I said as we stepped into the street. I pulled out a pack of cigarettes. "I smoke."

"Oh, God," he said. "That's terrible."

"I don't have to smoke all the time and there is such a thing as toothpaste," I said. "We've spent some serious time together in the last twenty-four hours and I haven't lit up."

"So why now? I'm leaving."

"Dunno. That movie. The low sky. Sunday evenings." I sighed but put them away.

We talked through our mutual tiredness in the two blocks to the subway, but I don't remember about what until Daisy got into a trash bag outside the butcher shop and came up with three (yes, really: *three*) baguettes. She looked like a rhinoceros that had gotten its horns and bumps mixed up. I was crying with laughter as I tried to pull them out and she deftly turned her head the other way. A man saw my struggle and started laughing, too. "Can I take a picture of that?" he asked.

He got my email address and left. I turned to Galean. "Thank you so much for brunch and hanging out with me."

"It was fun," he said.

"Let's talk soon."

He kissed me good-bye, one arm crooked around my neck. I walked my bread-bristling beast home with a smile. I'd had a couple of good dates. I was hoping for another one, with Galean, the next weekend. This was riches beyond riches and I was worried. If I found myself with a boyfriend, would I give up this book and settle for happiness?

Eight

Pandas lose interest in sex in captivity because they will only mate with pandas that have personalities like their own. At one time, scientists developed panda porn to stimulate male arousal, as well as dosing them with Viagra.

"You know the weirdest thing about him?" I said to Will. "He looks a lot like your Rico."

"My boyfriend or my Chihuahua?" he said with his Tin Man's creaky laugh.

"Boyfriend."

"Really," he exclaimed, his voice turning sharp. "Really" is one of those words that should be in the Urban Dictionary. I first picked it up from Janeane Garofalo and it seems to have gone viral. If you come down hard and sharp on the first syllable—reee—and nearly drop the last and use it as a one-word sentence, it mixes being impressed with irony, expectation with disbelief. It is one of Will's and my in-words.

"Send me, send me!"

I clicked around How About We and emailed his photo.

"Yeah, I can definitely see it. What kind of name is Galean?"

"Spanish. He's half Puerto Rican."

"He looks intense."

"He is, kind of. No guy's made me laugh as hard since Dar."

"If he can make you get over Dar, I love him already. When are you seeing him again?"

I yawned. "Not for days, I hope. I haven't stayed up that late and drunk that much and then followed up a couple of hours later with more booze and more talk in donkey's years. He's thirty, I need time to recover."

"Do you have his phone number? You should call him."

"I have it on caller ID but I want to play it cool."

"Nail him."

"He almost nailed *me*. He's an ass man."

Will purred. "Did you leave the deed undone?"

"I invoked the Third Date Rule, but I could change it to second for Galean."

He started laughing. "I got the picture of Daisy. 'Bread Dog.' What a hoot. She looks like a pincushion. Did she like *Galean*?" He pronounced his name in second-grade singsong. Pretty soon we'd be sittin' in a tree.

"Of course."

"Did he like Daisy?"

"I think so," I said slowly.

"He has to," he said firmly. "Anyway, how could he not? She's loving and funny and gorgeous."

"And big and the star of the show," I added. "You know, it's perfectly possible that having a big dog would be one of the first things that could attract me to a guy. It's weird that it doesn't seem to work the other way around, even though I make a point of her in my profiles and photos."

"It's New York, honey. And don't forget: You and I have the talent of enjoying dogs. Not everybody does. It's like a foreign language or something." I like how our lives mirror each other. He's an endocrinologist; I write about obesity. He's a veterinarian; I walk dogs even when I'm adjunct teaching. I feel like a prized Steuben miniature of him when we talk about those things.

I was pulling stuff together to go see my acupuncturist as I talked to Will, two months since Hero had tried to mix it up with the beagle, Bacchus, and twisted me around in ways a person shouldn't twist. The pinched nerve in my shoulder made my elbow sensitive to the air conditioner near my desk, and waves of numbness would wash over the left side of my chest and arm.

"Sounds like myocardial infarct," my father had said dispassionately. "You better get yourself to a doctor *now*."

It's a family joke that Dad, a retired doctor with a sixth sense for diagnosis, was serious about aches and illnesses when he A) hauled out antibiotics, or B) sent us to a doctor. I knew he was concerned when my brother called and told me to at least start taking aspirin every day.

But the numbness in my fingers, like the numbness in my heart, was starting to recede. I was walking Italian greyhounds, an elderly golden retriever and a French bulldog that summer. I could shake my left arm as much as I wanted while walking all that docility.

"All I can say is that Daisy was loving with Galean and that she eventually went to sleep in the bathroom."

"Ah, summer," Will said. "All three of my bulldogs are asleep on the kitchen floor. It's tiled, too."

I hurried to Dr. Chan's feeling comforted that Rico hadn't batted an eye when Will gave him Elodia, a bulldog bitch puppy. They already had six Pekingese, two grumpy Chihuahuas (including Rico, who was a biter) and a cat. Elodia came with a bulldog boyfriend lined up for her future fecundity, just to increase the joy, chaos and Pet Head shampoo when she had a litter of three. Some men aren't afraid of canine devotion.

Talking to Will made me realize how much I had to tell Galean. About my sardonic and rather brilliant father, about dog breeds and how to speak dog, about Will himself, about why I wanted to sleep on the left side of the bed. Being cupped by Dr. Chan. Janeane Garofalo. My students and the way early morning light pours like gray silk through the louvered windows into Grand Central concourse . . .

The vocabulary of dating is full of conditions and as I hunched on a massage chair with electrodes making my arm and hand jump, I thought about "when we ___" and "it'd be really fun to ___." Will was right. I should be in touch.

I emailed Galean when I got home, thanking him for my pop culture tune-up and for making me laugh, and I attached the photo of Bread Dog.

He replied that I was welcome and that work was busy.

Then nothing.

I couldn't bring myself to stalk him and so what conversation

we'd had up to and through the weekend turned into a mono-
logue of "maybe," "if only," "what did I ___?" "was I too ___?"
"should I/we have ___?"

I sucked it up so that my friends would think me brave. Celia
asked me round to share a bottle of wine and Carol talked up
JDate's over-fifty speed dating. Jean reminded me that this was
not a breakup. Will requested I find us a cabana boy and Kevin
upped it to three so that we'd each have one. Bette had the
picture of Bread Dog printed and framed for me. I put it on the
window ledge, above the air conditioner that made my elbow
ache. Daisy the carb-queen was lying on the love seat in front
of the air conditioner, asleep on her back with her front paws
dream-fluttering in the air and her back legs splayed shame-
lessly. She was eight inches away from where I was sitting.

You have friends, I told myself sternly. *A dog who lives to live with
you. You have interesting students and a book to write.*

You even have other guys wanting to correspond with you.

Yes, ma'am, I told that other half of myself, who talks a big
game but who I ignore on a regular basis.

Daisy and my two selves would be the only friends who'd be
around late on Saturday night.

*   *   *

Galean had produced the electric shock of making me laugh
until my cheeks hurt.

Laughter is electric with anyone. Because I am so often the
funny one, I can become a half-baked lesbian when a girlfriend

has me panting for the next zinger. But the amperage spikes when it happens between two people who suspect they'd like to get naked as soon as possible.

Laughter is ambidextrous sadomasochism. You're either surrendering or mastering.

The only thing I can think of to match laughter is the synchronicity that goes by the inept phrase of "getting it." That's what rips my heart out any time I think of Dar. Without speaking, he and I understood the backstory of a backstory. It was a club of two that made me want it to be Us Two.

"One of my favorite lines from Trollope," I mused one night at dinner with my parents and Dar, "is 'proud as piecrust.'"

My mother put her fork down and looked at me in consternation. "That doesn't make sense. I'm proud *of* my piecrust but . . ."

Dar and I widened our eyes and looked at each other.

"Maybe it's a matter of how well a piecrust stands up," he said. "Is it a . . . *stiff* crust, or mushy?"

His face was as red as a cherry turnover. I was biting my lower lip and shredding the napkin in my lap, fighting back a fit of giggles. Mom looked more confused than ever and Dad finally looked up from his plate and inspected our barely suppressed hilarity with a grunt that told us we were flagged and on our own for being so childishly smutty.

It was smut, but it was also my mother's long history of pie making and the puddly place in our tummies where we were being stupidly juvenile about Victorian novels as well as the real possibility that Dar would want my mother's recipe and

would be surprised and interested to learn that she was thinking of pumpkin pie when he was thinking of apple pie and I
was dreaming of black cherry pie, and that Dad has stories of
raisin pie at a hole-in-the-wall in Florence, Montana, but preferred the mincemeat he used to make with venison, which
would prompt me to give a little history lesson regarding mincemeat. And the moment would continue tomorrow when Dad
suddenly decided to make the custard if I made the crust. And
if I spoke or emailed Dar tomorrow, he'd wonder what kind of
pie Dad had been inspired to make before I mentioned it.

And so on, into the silly pink cotton candy of the future.

How do you put that craving into a personal ad?

*   *   *

So much back-and-forthing between two generations of regret—
Dar, Galean, Galean, Dar—made me sick of myself. Instead
of saying, "I like this, I like that" in my Big Beautiful Woman
Cupid profile, I blew off the questions about Hobbies/Interests.
Excluding "other," BBWCupid offers fifty-one choices under
Fun/Entertainment. If I were a guy, and a woman I liked the
looks of had checked off antiques, shopping, casino/gambling,
crafts, fashion events or collecting, I'd start looking for a different sort of dating site—Already Got A Life-dot-com, maybe,
or No Handmade Gifts. And I quickly backed up into cyberspace when I was confronted with a menu of men whose interests included motorcycles, bars/pubs, investment and karaoke.

And yet . . .

When I was a literary agent, I represented a gem of a memoir about rebuilding an Indian motorcycle and, in my hipster neighborhood with its banks of pastel Vespas, I have an intermittent fixation on photographing interesting bikes. A guy who mentioned a vintage Norton could score some points.

I have caveats for hobbies/interests. I tick off writing, for instance, but it's not a hobby. I love giving and going to dinner parties, but the Bat Cave doesn't have room for them, so I leave it blank. My computer and Internet are my most important possessions, but I don't in the least understand them. By "ballet," does Cupid mean doing or going to?

One of my caveats fell under camping/nature.

That phrase reminds me of all the dopey Girl Scout campouts I went on that pitted freezing and having to use an outhouse against the fun of s'mores and . . . s'mores. We'd go off to some campground and pitch our tents, and various teams gathered firewood or cooked or hauled water. It was camping for the sake of camping because I don't remember anything of the scenery except the woods.

The very keenest pleasure I had when I was thin, however, was hiking in Montana. My boredom level is low, so the harder, the better. I didn't speed-hike the way Lisa, my guide and niece, does. I took my camera, I got excited over mountain sorrel, I was astonished and sort of blessed by sharing space with mountain goats, I laughed at Daisy whipping along from ledge to lake to cliff. I'd be willing to camp in a heartbeat if it meant getting to see the unseeable—Lupfer Glacier or Roaring Springs Canyon. That is camping for the sake of privileged information.

How charmed I was when I received a long response from a gray-haired and neatly bearded man that noted, "There are so many good, intelligent lines in your ad that I feel foolish for singling out just one. It was when, in your sort-of discussion of sort-of camping, you use the phrase 'deeper into the beauty.'* That was lovely. I knew just what you meant."

The rest of what he had to say was tinged, a little sadly I thought, by diffidence. He assumed I was probably mobbed so he wouldn't hound me and if I wasn't mobbed I should keep looking for someone because there are good guys out there.

His modesty was dear but unnecessary.

> *Many are the times when I've wanted to edit my own ad to say, "If you have more than three garments in your closet with Disney characters on them [more than one if the character in question is Tigger] or if you refer to your breasts as 'boobs,' keep moving!" But I haven't. Yet.*

I laughed.

Any reasonable person knows that the *only* acceptable illustrations of the Pooh stories are Shepard's. There are very few reasonable people left when it comes to the classics Disney has cute-ified to the point of hyperglycemia.

I was impressed.

---

* Fourteen months after writing that ad, I have to say "deeper into the beauty" is a damn good line.

He handled the tricky comma-in-quotes-within-quotes with unusual aplomb.

I shivered.

"You look adorable. You also look happy. Happy women are almost always beautiful women: That is the great irony at the heart of dating."

My physical aspirations have always revolved around the word "adorable." *And* he used the adjectives "pugnacious" and "disingenuous," and managed to quote *A Midsummer Night's Dream* <u>and</u> *The Addams Family*.

I have never scrambled to reassure and encourage as fast as I did that morning to Jeremy.

He wrote immediately of his relief and his frustration with pissed off Big Beautiful Women who'd been burned by fat-hoppin' guys.* More to the point of his day, however, was that he had an article due for the audiophile magazine he was on the staff of. "Mostly I write about MAXX3 speakers so I'm excited to write about my favorite singer at the moment, Joanna Newsom. Do you know her?"

My stomach clenched at the thought of another Mackie-Messer-Lou, but he skipped right along to asking—*asking*, not

---

* "Mark," of practicalpickup.com, writes of how thin men "give in" to fat women for one-night stands: "With the right combination of depression, desperation and alcohol, any man can succumb to any woman, even if she looks like the Michelin Man." There is a new, inner ring of hell for Mark and his friends.

telling, and especially not telling and then asking—who my favorite poet was.

"One of my first teachers was Dick Hugo," I wrote back, "and he still gets to me."

"I'm rushing to pick up my daughter from school but I had to write you immediately. Of all the poets anyone could choose, I can't believe it was Richard Hugo. 'Dick.' My God. Such power. So many great lines: 'The day is a woman who loves you.' Who *are* you??"

It only took one word to answer that. He would Get It because it was the second sentence of the poem he had quoted:

"Open."

Welcome to Dar Country.

* * *

Except, of course, that Dar didn't have a sixth grader named Katie and a wife named Joan who was in a long-term passionate affair with a married man.

"We'll probably split up when Katie leaves home but it's an open marriage for now. I work from home so I do the housework and homework. Katie is my Best Girl."

Beware the father of a daughter, my superego said.

Shuddup, my id said, presenting the middle finger to my frontal lobe.

He lived in New Paltz and was a Girl Scout leader. *When does he plan to see you?*

Love will find a way, id hummed.

You're a sap, my superego said, and flounced off to plan a lesson on subordinating conjunctions.

I decided to heed the debate, at least a little. "Just how does an open marriage work?" I asked. "Have you had other relationships? Does your wife know?"

"I was seeing a woman I met on Cupid for about a year. We were very fond of each other but she met someone whom she could plan a future with. No hard feelings."

At least no hard feelings *after* she met someone who could sleep over.

"What about your wife?"

"I've opted not to tell her although I'm sure she knows. I mean, *I* know that when she takes her cell phone with her for a walk at night she's talking to him and that when she works late or goes away on business they're together. This wasn't my idea and I don't want to hurt her."

"You're a good man," I said. "A better man than I am a woman." My fist was clenched.

●　●　●

Here we are—Sol, Lou, Patrick, Paul, the Orange Rose Guy, Jeremy and me—in our fifties, outnumbered by our baggage. Not over the last relationship, a life of diffidence in obesity, the needs and joys of children, religion, working for the Man or making a living on a narrow margin, tastes crafted over forty years and many trials: We are a motley bunch and sometimes it feels as if our bags and bundles have been in our cellars for too long and the rooms themselves would make for an episode of *Hoarders*.

The same factors were present ten years ago but this mustiness and the feeling that we've forgotten half the junk stored away wasn't there. A man in his mid-forties seems to look forward to each date and the next girlfriend. If he has kids, they're young enough that he wants everyone to get along on a daily basis.

After the larkiness of Galean, Jeremy seemed to epitomize all that is best and worst about our decade. He was well-spoken, polished, passionate—and he was married.

And let's not forget the hardening of proclivities that comes with age. Like Lou, Jeremy liked "curvy" women. His wife was pillowy and his former girlfriend weighed 382 pounds.

Three hundred and eighty-two pounds??? my lately unwanted superego screeched.

"Wasn't that hard for you?" I asked.

"I've always liked big women. And no, my mother was thin."

"Wasn't it hard for her?"

"W-eee-ll," he considered. "She did have some trouble walking to the end of the block."

I flashed back to Patrick pushing corn bread at me. He'd have made sure she didn't get to the end of her driveway.

Then again, 382 pounds. Is it typical for men to describe their exes by specific weights before mentioning her hair color or her job or her sense of humor?

I'm still unnerved by this preference for big women. I've spent my life in the jail of my body size, whether I was fat or thin. I'm longing for some open space where I can simply be

Frances. Unless one is an anchorite devoted to the divine, I think it takes intimate relationships, of various sorts, to *be*. What's the point of making my amazing artichoke stew or watching the clouds take shapes if I don't have someone to serve or point it out to?

Our conversations meandered into what we were reading and Katie's birding project for Scouts and how he grills scallops. We laughed over my insistence that despite the political incorrectness of liking beef, I'd take prime rib over a scallop any day, and we laughed some more about Katie's cat that sat in front of her bunnies' hutches as if it were watching porn with surround sound.

The baggage was musty but we were getting a good chuckle out of the contents.

I hoped, despite Katie and Joan and the menagerie, that this was another aspect of dating in late midlife: that we have become aware that our entrenched lives are fodder for mockery.

. . .

We had three weeks of emails and sneak-away phone calls and a few confessions of what we wanted to do with each other and suddenly he was coming! Joan had decided to take Katie to visit her parents in Michigan and he was driving them to LaGuardia on Sunday afternoon.

My Hugo-quoting, Disney-hating, masturbating-over-me-at-night supreme optimist would be in Brooklyn Heights at dinnertime with a week of familylessness ahead of him.

Bette, Celia, Jean and Carol clucked so much I had a menagerie of my own going.

"If his marriage is open, wouldn't it make sense for his relationships to be open?" Caroline said, and I had to admit I'd hire her as my divorce attorney in a minute.

"Are you nuts?" Bette asked. "Do you have, like, an infinite number of feelings to get hurt?"

"Why don't you ask him to dinner with us?" Jean offered. "Ben will grill halibut; I'll grill Jeremy."

"If he doesn't want to hurt his wife's feelings," Celia said, "he doesn't want to change things. You, my dear, would be a change."

"Bring your jammies," I told Jeremy.

"It's August. Will I need them?"

"I don't have sex on the first date."

"Aren't you the coy thing?"

It was 90 degrees outside and the dress I'd worn to school was sticking to my legs. I shivered.

. . .

I shoved essays aside and began to clean. Cleaning the Bat Cave is harder than cleaning a ten-room house because it's jam-packed and everything has to be moved at least twice. I swept up dog grit before putting Swiffer to floor in the final attempt to not blacken my feet walking barefoot. What other cities call "dust" in New York is airborne dirt that resurrects itself daily, curling into discoloring smears on the cabbage of my miniature teapot and giving my stuffed penguin head a full pate of hair.

Fighting the tarry city air that stains the knobs on the stove and filters everything through weak lenses is boring, dirty, stupid work when I could be reading *The Black Cauldron* or poking Will in the ear with my pencil.

Wait. Sorry. The crud I moved around in the dank marshalling heat of August horniness made me jittery and prone to forgetting my keys and flashing back to the past. Perhaps plotting adultery amid the piles of essays, tumbleweeds of dog hair and sweat pooling on my back was addling my mind with guilt as well as expectation.

Because after and amid so much fruitless tomfoolery with weird men and men who didn't, quite, love me, I wanted to love, once again, someone who loved me back.

• • •

The house I love most is 70 Willow Street. I loved it first for the climbing roses spidering up its yellow brick walls and then because I learned that Truman Capote had lived there while waiting for the appeal results for Richard Hickock and Perry Smith. As a memoirist, I sympathize with Capote's dilemma of loving a man who needed to die in order to finish his book.

As a Brooklyn Heightsian, on the other hand, I am perturbed by people pointing and gawking. One day I walked by as the renter of the three-story mansion was planting impatiens in front. She looked wearily at me. I smiled and said, "He lived in the *basement*." She laughed, stood up and stuck out her hand. "I'm Kay. Who are you?"

We had a good giggle at what it's like to live in a minor shrine and discussed how the world has benefited from Capote's landlord, Leland Hayward, who produced *South Pacific* and *The Sound of Music*.

It was the first stop on my walking tour of Brooklyn Heights with Jeremy. I showed him the garden apartment filled with exercise equipment that had been Capote's actual home and then recounted my story of meeting the present owner.

I was in a cool perspiration of relief. He was a little taller than me, thin, with graying hair and beard, hipster glasses and a broadcloth shirt hanging out of his jeans. It's not that his photos were ugly, but I felt comfortable with his body and his style. I felt we fit, like two spoons that could coexist in a spoon nest.

I didn't feel fat as we walked down Orange Street. In my cotton skirt and red huarache slides, I felt tall and strong and smart. I pointed out the early nineteenth-century wooden colonial houses that have survived fires and nor'easters, described how the likes of Carson McCullers and Gypsy Rose Lee had scrummed together on the part of Middagh Street that was whacked off for the BQE, and asked questions about his garden and who was feeding the chickens that night. We backtracked to see the carriage house Marilyn Monroe and Arthur Miller shared, with an excursion to Montague Terrace to see the buildings W. H. Auden and Thomas Wolfe lived in. I was thrilled to show my little inspirations to someone who could appreciate them, but when I asked if he wanted to see the most darling street this side of Washington Square Mews, he looked at me as if I were crazy.

"It's really hot out," he said.

"Oh." It was and I felt it, but if the humidity isn't fuzzing the horizon, I try not to complain. "Do you want to go somewhere?"

"I'd like to get something to eat, if you don't mind."

"Not at all. What's your pleasure?"

We went into that rigmarole of what's-good versus what-are-you-in-the-mood-for and, finally, he opted for sushi.

Sushi. God's way of telling tuna they should have crawled out of the primordial muck with the arthropods.

I like my fish cooked and I have an unbreakable no sucker cups/no jet propulsion rule that pretty much leaves me with an artful display of California roll.

Then I remembered Bette's birthday at a local Asian restaurant, with balloons and crepe paper and silly hats and plates of Indian pancakes and vegetable tempura. They had actual food on their menu as well as eel, squid, skin and roe.

We were both grateful for the air-conditioning, and we gulped at our ice water. Despite the uncooked tides the chef was fashioning in colorful fastidiousness, Jeremy ordered broiled fish with steamed vegetables—ordinary food. I brightened and leaned in to concentrate on the ideas for books he wanted to run by me.

"One of the things that pisses me off the most is that cleaning products do the opposite of what they're supposed to," he said. "Take Pledge, for instance. It leaves a film that actually *attracts* more dust. What do you think about a book about how consumers are ripped off?"

I made my Thinking Face, the one where I sort of flatten my lips together in a long line that says, "Huh!"

"Well . . . I dunno," I stalled. "You have to think who your readership will be and where they get their information. There's *Consumer Reports* and the Web and *Hints from Heloise* readily available."

"I see what you mean."

Our meals came and we busied ourselves with cutlery while I searched for a way to spin his idea.

"I'd suggest alternative cleaning methods except that I have a set of books about using baking powder and salt that are close to that."

"This is the most phenomenal mackerel I've ever had," he said, changing the subject and looking up at me. His eyes were the color of old-fashioned, well-worn blue jeans.

"Really? I'm so pleased! I always worry when I pick a restaurant."

"Unbelievably good. I've got to try to make this for Katie."

"Maybe that's what you should write about: raising a fish-eating twelve-year-old."

He laughed. "Once we were driving home from a band concert in Kingston and I decided we'd stop for Kentucky Fried Chicken. I told her, 'This is why you have to grow up. So you can eat KFC any time you want.' Katie would be happy living at home for the rest of her life."

"My grand-niece is like that. She lives with her parents on

ten acres in Oregon and would be happy raising goats and rabbits and spinning yarn and looking up recipes online."

"We should introduce them. Angora or mohair?"

I smiled my rarest smile. I felt as on the verge of possibility as a cashmere kid finding its feet for the first time.

It was time to go meet Daisy.

I warned him how small my apartment is, that I have enough books to fill a Staten Island ferry, that even bright lights leave pockets of murk. I told him Daisy would rush to meet him and to expect a European exchange of kisses and that when he sat down, she would sit with him like a Park Avenue hostess tuned to the latest messenger of scandal.

I warned him.

He sat on the love seat and Daisy draped one paw over his shoulder and gave him a good sniffing over as he looked around.

"It's . . ."

". . . really small," I supplied.

"Yes. And really . . ."

". . . crowded?"

"How do you live like this?"

I like my stuff. It reminds me who I am on days when the Black Dog of depression has me in its jaws. I can't be *so* terrible if I've read all that Tudor history or have a *That Girl* Barbie next to a—oh, heavens. I hadn't dusted the nuns.

"I'm used to it. I focus so hard that I don't feel that confined. And Daisy is always within petting distance."

"Daisy is quite . . ."

I cocked my head. "Beautiful? Smart? Affectionate?"

". . . friendly."

The air quotes around the word crackled like distant thunder.

"Can I get you—?"

"Didn't you tell me about the view of the city from a park nearby? Let's go someplace less . . . doggy." He sniffed to underline his point.

It was near sunset and the Promenade was exactly where we should be.

We ambled south, far enough along to see the Empire State and Chrysler Buildings, in companionable silence. The sun was turning the world behind us apricot. The Promenade was thronged with tourists and tripods, parents and strollers, toddlers in pajamas eating ice cream. We stopped to watch the gravid sun hover on the New Jersey horizon.

"This has been good," I said.

"It has," he agreed. "I enjoy talking to you."

"Me, too."

"And getting to see Brooklyn Heights. It's pretty here. I didn't know you could be this close to Manhattan and be almost bucolic."

I smiled. I liked the word "bucolic."

"I'd like to know more of you," he continued. "And yet . . ."

I turned to him.

"I don't feel It. I thought I would. You're wonderful and smart and funny and pretty, but I don't feel It. The Thing. You know."

Of course I know.

"Let me show you back to the parking garage."

We trudged four blocks in silence. I blinked back tears until we got to the mouth of the garage.

"It was great," he said. "I'd like to—" He finally looked up at me. I held out my hand, said, "Drive safely" and watched until he was swallowed by the cave of the car park.

Three hours earlier I had walked beside a man of poetry and music and ripening corn and I'd felt long-legged and sure and keen. Now, as soon as he was out of sight, I went into Gristedes. Daisy will fill the bed just fine, I told myself.

Especially if I have Mission to Marzipan ice cream and Stella Dora almond cookies.

Nine

The orchid releases a chemical that makes bees drunk. When the bee becomes disoriented, it dumps its load of pollen into the flower, thus pollinating the flower.

The Galean-Jeremy-Mission-to-Marzipan hangover wasn't pretty. I taught my classes, came home and read chick lit novels, finishing one and downloading another onto my Kindle before I could so much as roll over in bed. I looked for clues in them, but mostly I wanted the formula: kooky girl with the wrong guy changes her career and man. I shunned my friends and sank into cynicism. When Caroline called to sign me up for the JDate Speed Date, I responded with a sour joke. "Do you know that a whale's penis is called a dork? So which came first, the dork or the dick?"

She laughed but said, "I wouldn't share that with a bunch of nice Jewish men, if I were you."

"You know how Nora Ephron defined a Jewish Prince? He

comes into the living room and says, 'Honey, do we have any ice cubes?'"

"It's attitude, Frances. You gotta have the right attitude."

"Uh-huh. So what's your excuse for being fifty-three years old and never married?"

Carol told me later that they had a good time at the speed date. A banker and a real estate agent asked for Caroline's number and Meg met a college girlfriend whom she got tipsy with.

I turned to Will for his post-mortem on my most recent dating debacle.

"I feel for ya, France," Will said, "but think of it this way. You came close. You actually met some guys you liked for a change."

"Great," I said. "That and two-fifty will get me to St. Patrick's Cathedral. I can light a candle for my slutty, messy, adulterous soul."

"Are you an adulterer if you're not married?" he asked. "I think Jeremy was the one who contemplated mortal sin."

"The thing about you men," I began to pronounce, "is that you can't take it step-by-step with a prospective partner. You know, you meet and you like her but not sexually. But you have a lot to talk about or things you could do together and have fun. Maybe you talk some more and see each other some more and find yourself falling in love. I haven't said no to a second date in years because of that."

"What really went wrong, France? Think. You had a great time with Galean. You laughed and you fooled around. Then nothing. What happened between fooling around and nothing?"

I was quiet, reconstructing that afternoon. Daisy wanted to

be part of the petting. We were tired and evening was coming on so we walked him to the subway. I smoked a cigarette.

"Jeremy was annoyed by Daisy, too. He made a comment about the dog hair getting to his allergies. He has a cat, for God's sake! How could he be allergic to dog hair?"

"Allgery-schmallergy," he said. "That's why God invented Claritin."

"I don't think he liked the Bat Cave."

"The Bat Cave is *fine*."

"He complained about the heat. It was a hot day. I was running him all over the Heights showing him stuff."

"Maybe he doesn't want to be with a woman who can walk past the end of the block."

"Oh. My. God. You mean, I was too . . . thin?" I was choking with laughter.

"You've picked some winners, Frances."

. . . .

He was right, although not quite in the way he meant it. Galean and Jeremy were good guys, but I was wrapped up in the role I was auditioning for: finding a happy ending. I cleaned my apartment—for men. I had my hair and eyebrows done—for men. I talked about the books they might want to write and prayed my musical taste would pass muster and that Daisy would behave. For men.

Bull. Shit. Daisy always behaves. She behaves like Daisy. Craven in her greed and reactions, and completely egocentric.

I have a vast collection of music that I love. I didn't need Galean or Lou or even Dar to approve what I listen to.

Dar. Back to Dar. Dar hadn't minded the dog hair or the Bat Cave or Daisy wrapped around his leg humping him for dear life. I missed him. In the weeks of Galean and Jeremy, with my hopes high, Dar wasn't on my heart. When my hopes were dashed, it was back to Dar-this and Ben-and-Jerry-that. I was back to feeling rejectable.

Here's what Bette was right about: *I* picked this stage to reveal myself on and I was bleak and empty after three months of treading the boards.

But maybe I didn't need a guy. Maybe I needed me.

* * *

Time passed. Enrollment plummeted and I was no longer teaching. Dog walking was once again keeping me afloat while I dithered about finishing my novel or going out on the Modern Language Association career job hunt. If I got a job, what about Kevin and the farmette? How could I credibly say that teaching is a talent as innate as being able to carry a tune and that teaching is standing in front of a class in order to create a cocktail hour in which they can learn something through themselves, the work, each other, me? Hell, I consider myself a success when I can get them to use "its" and "it's" properly.

Despite adjuncting, I had stopped fitting into the mainstream of anything years ago, maybe when I got a job in publishing instead of finding a doctorate program in creative writing. I think I know more about the real world than most creative writing teachers do, but I didn't play the game my teacher Richard Hugo called po-biz.* Was that failure or boldness?

Maybe luckily, I found myself beset with dogs when a colleague took a two-week vacation. That September was murderously hot and humid and I couldn't find anything in my arsenal of walking shoes that was comfortable. After two days, I had angry purple blisters between my toes. I sterilized a needle at my gas stove, hopped to the bathroom and closed my eyes before piercing them. *Dang*, I thought. I wrote a dog-walking column for a local blog and I don't think I covered blisters in my "What Hurts Today?" piece. At least not bloody blisters. But back then I didn't have days that started at 7:30 a.m. and ended at 8:00 p.m.

There was one spell of a few hours, between 8:15 and 10:30, when I could have breakfast, write a few emails and allow myself some cynical charm by a highly poetic email romance with a man I'll call Dream Catcher. Like a bottle of cold water on these hot, humid fall days, he was oozing sensuality:

> *a rampage of fireflies*
> *shatters my heart,*
> *shatters my reason, burns—*

---

* Short for poetry business. I began my writing life as a poet. That's why, when I don't know what to do in a paragraph, I describe the sky.

until you drown me, moon-washed
river of all desire

In those mornings, and in the few minutes I had between gigs in the afternoon, we flirted, the poetry getting cheaper by the day.

Dream Catcher was married. He and his wife apparently couldn't stand each other but he wouldn't leave her because his kids were getting to the age of having their own children and their loyalty to their mother would prevent him from being a grandpa. Also, divorce was financially crippling.

Before I got completely exhausted from this new schedule of dogs, I was stupid enough to be aroused and to admit it. Here's a lesson I don't want to put in bold letters: When a woman cuts to slang in referring to her nether-regions, men start foaming at the mouth with lust. He begged to come over one morning, any morning, to make love to me.

But those mornings I was already beaten by the 90 degrees of high humidity I'd be facing in a couple of hours. My erotic thoughts dwindled. It was hard to write poems about picking up after a greyhound with a tummy ache.

His emails laughed when I explained. He would tend my wounds. He would take care of me for two hours a week, right after he got back from a family vacation in the Green Mountains.

But I didn't want to be tended. I wanted to go to Gettysburg and make love in a four-poster bed in a two-hundred-year-old bed-and-breakfast. I wanted to go to the movies, do sloppy quiet things during *Crazy Stupid Love* and then go drink coffee and talk about it after.

And that was what he couldn't give me. He couldn't even consider that, knowing me better, he might want to give me those things.

I could kind of understand his hopes of finding a mistress. He was my age and had been talking to/saving for/arguing over/sleeping with one person for thirty years. Thirty years! As often as not, a thirty-year-old person has his/her *own* kids and a mortgage and a specific career. Whole lives can mature in the course of thirty years—and whole lives can be disassociated. Living in a husk of a marriage would be as miserable as falling in love with a married man who wants to visit my bed at eight in the morning, on his way to work.

But if Mrs. Dream Catcher wasn't unhappy enough to go looking for a new shaman she could call her own, then she wanted to keep the marriage intact. His infidelities were the exponential echoes of the anger and pain a divorce would cost her.

There may truly be such a thing as an open marriage, but not if there are children and not if opening it was only one partner's idea. And it can close with a clap as sudden as a catfight.

For the sake of argument, then, a good rule of thumb is, simply, no married men.

* * *

Another rule, closely related: A man must have his own place. Unless you're much more Spartan and compulsive than I am, it's not fair that the onus of cleaning is placed completely on the woman. Especially if she has a dog.

• • •

After that devilishly hard two weeks ended, it occurred to me that I might invite Dream Catcher over on a Thursday morning. I had fewer dogs on Thursday; I could force myself to get it together to clean the bathroom, scoop up the worst of the dog hair and put clean sheets on the bed. But Dream Catcher could not, when I told him about my dogs and deadlines, see that those are the *who* of me, the answers I gave Kevin last night when he asked how I am. Busy. Tired. Excited. Stressed. Amused. That moon-washed river is his *what* of me. Italian greyhounds and the book review for a friend that I was keen to post on Amazon interested him only insofar as they interrupted his fantasy or whether I could whisper them in bad blank verse.

The detritus of my life is meaningful to Kevin and he doesn't forget it from one day to the next. When it's his turn to fret at feelings of emptiness I ask him what's in bloom on his balcony or what he's making for dinner for his sponsor.

Dream Catcher couldn't open up the who of himself. I suggested that Provolone cheese and the rain forest humidity we were enduring were fit topics of conversation and he disagreed. "I am much more ready to reveal myself in pillow talk than to do so on a walk or on the phone, which has never had an appeal for me—it is like sex in utter darkness—there is more mystery and stimulation where there is some degree of visibility at least. It's just the way I've learned I am."

Sounds like a really lonely life to me. I deleted the exchange and headed out to pay my Verizon bill and splurge on wild fresh salmon at Garden of Eden. Ben's birthday was coming up and I wanted to make something he loved. This, I thought as I walked up Montague Street, is what life is. Knowing someone well enough that I don't have to think twice about what to take to his birthday dinner, then going home to research Regency furniture for my novel.

Interestingly, forty-eight hours later Dream Catcher emailed again, not to plea through a sonneteer's seductions but to say it would have been better to meet by chance in an innocuous place and wondered whether I was making progress toward my writing deadlines. I was presented with yet another rule: Be yourself, no matter how fey you seem. If he wants to know you, he'll back off his initial terms. If doesn't, he wants a sex toy made to order.

Despite having enjoyed my brief experiments in being a sex toy, I'm not one, because I want to be known, I want to feel more myself through someone else, I want to risk more than an STD.

All Dream Catcher had to do was keep reading craigslist and Ashley Madison to find a housewife in the same loveless predicament he was in who would adore the romance of poetry.

He didn't need me. And that was the saddest fact about all the men I'd dated. They may not have liked me, or I them, but at least it had been personal. The salt taste of you, the rosemary sweat in the dark corners of you, are as impersonal and as little to do with Frances Kuffel as a fund-raising letter from the Republican Party.

* * *

Fairy tales, dogs, reclusion, having to resurrect myself from the last binge of mood or food folded me into origami as I sat, fittingly, outside Studio 54 with my head buried in my snot-covered hands. I'd summoned the courage to do the "I'm my own best friend" thing and go to see *Sondheim on Sondheim*. I thought I'd see some new songs and listen to old favorites. Instead, I watched a musical version of the hatchet job I've been doing trying to chop through to my better self.

I will risk egregious simplicity and state that Sondheim's musicals have one great unifying theme: the marrow-deep hunger to step from observer to participant, whether it is in love or in art. "Maybe you could show me how to let go, lower my guard, learn to be free"* repeats itself through the selections in *Sondheim on Sondheim*. The great sadness is that so often it is the articulation of the epiphany of wanting that is a show's dénouement. Bobby wants to be alive by the end of *Company*, but he'd only begun to search for a way to do it. In *Passion*, Fosca, too, finds she wants to live—as she is dying.

And in the meantime, there is aching, lyrical yearning through living vicariously. "I read to live," Fosca sings, and I winced at the surrogacy and escapism that have brought me a good vocabulary and much dusting to do and not much else.

---

* "Anyone Can Whistle" from *Anyone Can Whistle*.

"How you watch the rest of the world/From a window," George Seurat says of his two years' labor to catch a single moment, "While you finish the hat."* Was he most alive when the vision of the painting came to him, or in the absorption that is a loss of self that overtook him in the work that followed? "All of them good," Hollis sings of his artistic talents that have disappointed him, "but few of them better, none of them best,"† and I cringed with regret.

I remember how, in fourth grade and filled to the brim with my father's collection of Columbia House musicals, it made perfect sense to me to blurt into song over almost anything. If Eliza Doolittle could rant in song, why couldn't I do math class as a musical?

The first movie I remember seeing is *Carousel*. When left to story time and prayers, my father sang "Thank Heaven for Little Girls" to me. One sister-in-law's first memory of me was of hopping around the living room singing "I Feel Pretty."

I identified with musicals because you can sing along with someone else's life in a way that you can't mouth the lines of a play or movie or book. Will introduced me to *Company* in 1975 and I was finally able to articulate my ambition and lovelessness. I felt less alone when I belted out "Ladies Who Lunch" with Elaine Stritch.

---

* "Finishing the Hat" from *Sunday in the Park with George*.

† "Talent" from *Road Show*.

I was singing my life.

Which is how I chose the perfect date with myself and ended up on Fifty-fourth Street with a fist of pea-size Kleenex, taking stock of what it meant to be a single fifty-three-year-old who owns nothing, scraping by through spotty adjunct teaching and walking dogs, knowing my options for retirement are Ernest Hemingway's or Virginia Woolf's.

Of all those gorgeous songs and stories, *Sunday in the Park* reduces me to rubble. I told Will this when I described the show. He thought a moment and said, "My life is *Company*. I have to be with a man."

How strange, this reversal. At eighteen it would have been the other way around. That day, I felt emptier hearing that having a lover was the most important thing in his life. I wanted it but didn't understand how to get it.

And yet.

As much as I identify with the crisis of whether I can carry off a writing project and ache at the thought of what to do next, maybe Will is right about *Company*. If I was feeling like a lover was impossible, wasn't I slowly dying of the lack of what Bobby was drowning in:

Private names,
All those
Photos
Up on the walls—*

---

* Stephen Sondheim, "Company," *Company*, 1970.

• • •

That's what it's really about, right? My best friend forever lives 1,500 miles away. Kevin is 3,000 miles west. I had a social life on the street—all the people I know through dogs and with whom I exchange various degrees of intimate news—and two homes in my neighborhood where I might be found hanging out. Photos I took of Ben's mother and Jean and Ben's dog are up on the wall. We've sat up Googling national anthems until after midnight and Jean and I know each other's siblings well without ever having met them. Nan and I walk our dogs together and I always give her some kind of nutcracker for Christmas because I know she loves them.

If I could multiply Nan, Jean, Ben by 3.333333 and add a couple of casual boyfriends in the mix I might have all those private names, too—Francie, Francie baby, Franny, Fran, Frances darling, Frances, Frank-o . . .

That's what it's really about, along with the inversion of Bobby's problem: He'd met and left so many women who could have been Miss OK, while I'd met and been disregarded by so many men I still think might have been Mr. Perfect.

In "Someone Is Waiting," Bobby thinks of all his married women friends and asks the woman who has aspects of each to wait for him. I think of all the men who have brought me to my knees or worse when they liked but didn't love me or when I wasn't valuable enough to hang on to.

I took the time today to make a list of those men who touched me deeply. At the age of fifty-four, I have had eleven such men who have threatened or promised—oh, shit, I wish I could write this as well as Sondheim:

> *Someone to crowd you with love,*
> *Someone to force you to care,*
> *Someone to make you come through,*
> *Who'll always be there,*
> *As frightened as you*
> *Of being alive,*
> *Being alive.**

. . .

You know about Dar, and to be fair, Will loves me, now, as much as I now love him. The first boy who made me aware of being a girl was Joey Wade, who was in Sr. M. Marcella's first grade class with me. Was it my mother or his who decided we'd make cute sweethearts? All I remember is that he had a fire truck cake for his birthday party and I felt important and imposed upon, mixed up together, to be his girlfriend.

Joey left St. Anthony's after first grade and is notable only for that first awareness that Will would bring into crashing, hormonal brilliance six years later.

So that's eight men left. Eric, as eHarmony pointed out, has

---

* Stephen Sondheim, "Being Alive," *Company*, 1970.

never, quite, left my orbit. I think he would want to be best friends except that part of me hates him and another part of me is too ashamed to have much to do with a man I loved when I was a size six.

The man I loved in my thirties, Andrew, suggested, when I confessed that I was in love with him, that we get married—to other people and then tell each other about it. Even I had more dignity than that, but I've looked for him on the Web over the years and finally ran him to earth on LinkedIn.

"He lives in Salt Lake and he's so gray!" I told Grace. "And buttoned to the neck." I met Andrew through Grace when she was dating him in college. It was between graduate school stints that I planned our family and named our children.

"You don't think he's become a Mormon, do you?" she asked.

"I don't think Fichte and Joseph Smith would be two of the people one would want to meet in heaven," I said slowly. "But it's weird, you know, because he wrote me that he just finished a study of Fichte—in German—but he's all capital letters on his skill profile—SOS and BTW and whatnot, all to do with advanced computing. He has two daughters and some big career and he's still reading Fichte. Which is the real Andrew?"

I could hear Grace clicking on her computer. "His Facebook picture shows him with a young woman. Must be his daughter."

"Please tell me she's fat."

"She's beautiful."

"Then tell me her name isn't Claire or Margaret."

"He doesn't say."

So maybe our ghost children are intact and waiting for another incarnation. He was pleased to hear from me and asked what I was reading lately (hence the brief Fichte exchange), but I've given up being smart since leaving publishing. I was rereading the Harry Potter series at the time and I was embarrassed enough that I didn't get around to answering the email.

Maybe there will be no incarnation for Andrew and me.

I found several other men I'd had damaging crushes on through Facebook and LinkedIn. I'd Googled and scrubbed Facebook for years looking for the boy I dreamed about in high school (yes, I'm a slut: I could be in love with Will, see the writing on the wall and have a simultaneous serious pash for another boy), Shawn Eyre. With a name like that, I didn't understand why every girl in our class wasn't in love with him. Shawn was everything I wasn't. National Merit Finalist. Government. As normal as apple pie.

I finally realized he didn't spell his name "Shawn" and found him easily on LinkedIn, which seems to have more of us Boomers than Facebook.

He wrote back immediately, with curiosity and proper punctuation, telling me he lived in Seattle and was getting married for the first time in six months.

"Sean Eyre??" Will nearly shrieked. "You never told me that."

"I only really got to know him when we were seniors. You and I weren't speaking that year."

"I always remember him as sort of . . . a gentle soul." Will probably thinks of me as a gentle soul, along with Genghis Khan (*He was really passionate about his life*) and George W. Bush (*He always reminds me of a Havanese. They're the most loving dog I know*). This had never been my impression of Sean, whom I thought of as kind of forced to excel by his parents, who were in the snooty Missoula circle my parents could be found in if the cause was right. Maybe Will saw the what and I saw the why of Sean. That could sum our friendship skills up neatly.

"Whatever," I snipped. "Don't you see the cruelty here? I've never been married. He's never been married. I'm going to move to Seattle someday. He lives there now. I came *this* close. God hates me."

"I can see why you're disappointed."

"You know what he said about you and me?" I laughed bitterly. "He remembers how comfortable we each were in our own skin."

Will laughed as bitterly as I. "Yeah, I was this faggy artsy type and half the time I was living on other people's couches."

"And I was a two-hundred-forty-pound underachiever going through serious depressions no one recognized and I couldn't find panty hose that came up to my waist."

"If he thought we were so at home being weird, can you *imagine* how he must have felt?"

I was quiet at that because I couldn't, in fact, imagine it. No wonder he'd said he wasn't in touch with anyone from Missoula except his family.

I found I had to be careful with Sean. It was a little too exciting to hear from him, I had a little too much fear about emailing him, waited too ardently for a reply. He recommended a couple of books that were terrific and mentioned a hilarious "Shouts & Murmurs" piece, and I tended to make idiotic spelling errors out of nervousness. He was a Dar sort of Andrew, a Will-ish Eric, shelf material. Better off behind crystal wineglasses I never use.

•   •   •

As I walked dogs and listened to Sondheim scores on my iPod, I reckoned up that about half the men who'd made me feel, as Bobby in *Company* said, alive, still liked me. At least, they did once I tracked them down. Excluding Joey and his fire truck cake, the other half make up a group I decided was like Sweeney Todd's reaction to the beggar woman: "Off, I said! To the devil with you!"*

Daily Formetti might not have cast me off—I don't remember. Through him, I met the boy I went out with my junior year in college and who has a name so common I'll simply call him John Doe. John and I broke apart (versus "up") when he got sober. A year or two later I received an amends letter from him to which I responded bitterly, and I received no further communication from him.

I can't track a John Doe with no other information than the University of Montana in the late '70s, and Daily is dead. Daily taught me one good lesson: Don't fall in love with a priest. He

---

* Stephen Sondheim, "No Place Like London," *Sweeney Todd*, 1979.

should have reinforced what I learned at eighteen from Will: Don't fall in love with gay men.

But what could I do? Of these ten men, I actually fell in love at first sight with two of them, Daily and Eliot. Both of them were gay. Which is the more important lesson here—don't fall in love with gay men, or love at first sight does not work out? It's been thirty years since I fell in love on a first meeting, and it will add greatly to my happiness if I never do so again. No one needs that kind of tension in her life.

Let's be very, very precise about this: I was into Eliot the first time we met (on the phone, as it happens), but I was never in love with him. I wanted to *be* him. Even more than Sean, he'd had the charmed life I was too much of a fuckup to have crafted for myself. This was no flannel-shirt-and-*Liza with a Z* fag hagism, it was Thomas Mann, Tchaikovsky and von Gloeden hagging, with a dash of Bronski Beat when we went sightseeing. I can name twenty writers, composers and directors that are part of my life's blood that Eliot introduced me to. He had a grand, expansive, adjective-ridden brain and a lovely academic curriculum vita: the right undergraduate college, the right graduate school, tenure track at a fine college where he remains to this day, his first novel published while I floundered in my five minutes in a PhD program.

To be a true fag hag is to give up everything except what one's fag handpicks from one's arsenal of qualities, talents, abilities, and adding what one's fag finds missing. Eliot is the only gay man I have done this for and my motto in those years was "Heaven doesn't want me and hell's afraid I'm going to take over." We were, in the end, performance art, and performance art is fleeting. If it has any permanence, it's in photographs or memory. Perhaps I should be proud of the fact that I found permanence, lampooned in that first novel published in the years I struggled to get over him.

This book is predicated on my quest to replace Dar: Replacement is a tool I've used before. Becoming absorbed in Andrew allowed me to rearm myself, to get beyond the woman who was abandoned to shreds of self on a dance floor in Provincetown.

I can Google Eliot any time I want, but it still stings, his successes versus what a fuckup I feel. Recently, though, in my ongoing attempt to get rid of stuff in anticipation of leaving Brooklyn, I read a novel his editor gave me back in the days of being a literary agent. It is a mid-career novel. I thought it would be as quick a read as his first and that I would soon put it out one fine weekend day, to join all the other giveaways that make their way on to the balustrades and stoops of the Heights, a veritable free book fair.

I was wrong.

I got to the middle of the book just as it was time to walk a dog and without thinking, I said to Daisy, "I don't like this person very much." I had just read a scene in which a professor at a community college mangles a conversation about Isobel Armstrong with a male student. "Why *wouldn't* a community college student find Armstrong difficult to handle?" I complained to Daisy, who was looking hopeful that my new restlessness foretold a walk or maybe a trip to the dog run. "What kind of elitist *is* this author?"

I looked at her watching me with her intelligent amber eyes and realized I wasn't riffing on Eliot. He had become a separate entity from the man I'd boozed with and bought marionettes for thirty years ago.

I've taught that level of college for half of those thirty years. I know that student and I know the courage he and the others had that Eliot shrugged dismissively at in the novel. It's damned fucking *hard* to be the first generation to say, OK, I give up: I'll go to college and I'll take the required courses that are going to screw with my head because I've never thought about contractions or what Emily Dickinson means when she writes, "As cool to speech as stone." Eliot can write brilliantly about Beckett but he doesn't know shit about tickling the kid whose biggest dream is to own a boat into caring about something not bound between magazine covers.

Eliot hated musicals. He scoffed at them. They were some of those things I didn't bring up around him because they broke our hag code. But how far is *South Pacific* from *Madama Butterfly*, really? It's community college compared to Yale, but I'm willing to bet a lot of Yalie PhDs are out there teaching community college.

And didn't Sondheim go to Yale?

• • •

Which leaves one man on that list, Gregory McCarthy, who is also the person most likely to really understand my raucous, doomed ballet with Eliot. Greg was straight, but more bookish and, most important, more theatrical than anyone I know. He'd understand about fag hagging and he'd understand why Bernstein is as shattering as Gounod. Gregory and I fell in love with each other . . . but at different times. I requested his friendship on Facebook but he didn't respond. His page didn't look much used, but I only have that silence to go on. I'm sure he would tell you I hurt him—as his literary agent and as a woman who wanted him to be the writer Eliot is, I should accept that accusation. No one enjoys her guilt as much as I do, but for whatever reason, I don't accept it with Gregory. He got married, seems to have a going writing life and is beloved in his hometown, the metropolitan area of which is over five million people. Whatever hurt or setback I caused him, he has plenty of compensation. I have Daisy and thirteen dogs to walk. I deserve a five-minute pity party except that, the lack of a Facebook connection aside, I don't think about Gregory much.

I can't think about any of these men for very long without feeling the pinch of rejection and, with some of them, competition. John Doe, Eliot and Gregory cut me off at the knees, while Dar, Sean, Andrew and Eric unsettle me too much. I felt enough kinship with Eliot, Gregory and Dar that they feel like phantom limbs or a fifth, bloodless chamber of the heart.

Into the Woods begins with two words: "I wish." It is a cautionary tale about going into the black forest in order to find the right way to love. Looking at the roster of men I have been truly foolish over, I can see I did not choose wisely—if love is a choice. I walked around with my ears full of "A Little Night Music," daring Richard Strauss to out-magic "Perpetual Anticipation," and wished I had a man to love and love me back, such a simple, human thing. I couldn't choose the love me back part, but I didn't have to waste time over drugs, Brahmins, alcohol and needing the sanity of the exact opposite of Johann Fichte either. Not wasting time is part of adulthood. But I'd gotten stuck in the forest with my wishes and my history and there was a terrible chance I was neither a grown-up nor alive.

Ten

Albatrosses take an eighteen-month break between mating seasons, in which some fly around the world once. Others twice.

"When did this start?" Dr. Rosenblatt, my psychiatrist, asked. I'd been seeing her for my meds for the last ten years or so and it was a relief to get away from Dr. A-Cigar-Is-Not-a-Cigar, who always wanted me to talk to my child-self. I needed help and I needed it *then*. "Progress" was not an option in my current state.

I could pinpoint the exact events. The disappointment over Jeremy, followed by an epoch of self-pity stemming from my inventory of failure. In those couple of weeks, everything except ice cream began to taste like tin and the world oozed humidity and gray. That was the bad news. The worse news was that I'd been assigned two composition classes and had to suck it up four days a week to act like I knew what I was doing. It was agony.

"I think your meds have stopped working," my psychiatrist said. She got up to study my file. "How's your memory?"

I sniffed back the next sob and thought a moment.

"I-it's hard to say. Depression kind of effaces everything." Still, I'd been on a run of forgetting my keys, finding myself in the kitchen with no idea why, wondering what I'd worn the day before, a constant break in sentences while I searched for a word.

"Zoloft can affect memory but it will come back. You've been on a high dose for eight years. This is as bad as I've seen you since you first came and we started the Zoloft. Sometimes this happens. It's nothing to worry about, Frances."

Worry? I'd gone from *Company* to *Sweeney Todd* in two months, from wanting to feel alive to aching for a razor in my hand. I looked out her small window that faced a couple of dozen other small windows in the backs of the surrounding buildings. The gloom was the same every time I came here. It had taken me a couple of weeks to call her after I put a checkup on my to-do list. It was around Halloween that I found myself thinking things like, "I need to get coffee, stevia and kill myself." It's as close to psychosis as I've ever come because it didn't feel like I was generating those thoughts. They appeared, like a hungry blackbird left behind by the flock in its fall migration.

"If . . . anything, you know . . . happened to me," I asked Will in a shaky voice, "you'd take Daisy, wouldn't you?"

"You're depressed, aren't you, Francie?"

"Not really. I just want to make sure Daisy has backup."

"Well, she doesn't from me," he said angrily. "I'll give her to a kill shelter."

I began to cry. "Honey," he coaxed. "Daisy loves you the

same whether you're depressed or not. Just like me. You're going to get through this."

I wasn't so sure.

"I know it's hard, Sis, but you can't do that to me." Jimmie had inherited a Maltese along with his mother-in-law's decline into assisted living that came on top of taking care of our father for the half a year he spends in Montana.

There was no one else I would either talk about my depression with or ask for help if something happened.

If it wasn't about Daisy's future, I couldn't talk anymore. I couldn't bother Kevin, who was busy with school and working hard to stay sober. Even if I could put words to my feelings, they would surely make him want to drink. I'll wait until I have something to tell him, I told myself, but the world only got grayer and darker and colder.

And Daisy, until Dr. Rosenblatt pinned the problem on Zoloft, was the main thing I worried about.

She described how I would titrate off Zoloft, a drug with hideous withdrawals, onto Prozac, the first antidepressant I'd taken, way back in the early '90s. "We decided against Prozac when you first came in because one of its side effects is loss of libido," she warned me.

I laughed harshly. The last thing I needed was a libido.

"How bad off am I?" I wanted to know. It's easy to give into diagnoses, second dates, my clothing size, the number of Christmas cards I receive in order to know who I am.

She hesitated. "I don't want to minimize what you're going through," she said carefully. "But you have to remember I have patients who need to be hospitalized, to have ECT. I would say you're going through a medium depression."

I smiled to myself. Maybe I was already getting better because my own diagnosis was a lot different. If I'd had the money or insurance, and someone to take care of Daisy, I'd be first in line and waving my hand for admittance to the Cuckoo's Nest.

·   ·   ·

On the Sunday of Thanksgiving weekend, one of my best students—a flawlessly beautiful Scandinavian who had an A average in my class and sat with a bevy of other smart, beautiful friends from home—climbed over a ten-foot wire fence and jumped twenty stories.

Kadlin Ahlquist, at the age of twenty-one, effectively ended that errant voice in my head. I found myself wondering to my class about whether I should have discussed my depression with them. I was angry that the young woman who sat smiling serenely in front of me for five hours a week, who had everything, could throw her future away, could throw the faith of her friends, family and teachers away.

But I admired her, too. She was determined. She didn't make a mess for her roommates to find and deal with. She had kept this despair to herself, uncomplainingly. On Thursday she brought chocolate cake to the potluck Thanksgiving dinner with her fellow Nordics, and seventy-two hours later the group reassembled in shock.

"If anyone thinks Kadlin had a good idea, I will personally

come to your apartment and smack you," I threatened my class of twenty-year-olds. They cried as I cried, shocked that someone was talking about such violent feelings. When we were hauled into a counseling session straight out of a high school parody, I spoke when they would not, then heard my words parroted back when the counselors forced answers from students. "I want to know," a Norwegian hipster fumbled, "you know, when—like she"—he nodded at me—"said, when will it not be the first thing I think about when I wake up in the morning."

"No one can tell you that," one of the counselors said, and I wanted to stamp my foot and retort, "For everyone who was not a roommate or best friend, ten days. For the others, a month or two. You can start counting down now."

I believe in such lies. Stated authoritatively enough to kids who are desperate enough, they can become truth.

Later, when she called to ask if the Prozac was kicking in, Dr. Rosenblatt congratulated me. "Kids that age don't have the vocabulary to express the finer points of their emotions. You gave them the words they needed."

I tried. That seems often to be my job: giving people words. When a counselor called to discuss an incomplete for one of Kadlin's friends I was both sympathetic and adamant about the need for the right words.

"We're working hard to keep these kids in school and safe," she said.

"You want to do that? Call in the staff from the Swedish Seaman's Church." It is one of their gathering places, where they can indulge in comfort food and meet new people.

"Really? You think they would appreciate religious guidance?"

"No. I think they'd appreciate talking about it in *Swedish*."

*   *   *

I don't trust the words I answer myself with. "If I was my best friend, what would I tell me?" has gotten me in trouble by saying things like, "Of *course* you need ice cream. It's been a terrible day" or "Invite him over. It'll be an experience." I wish I had someone as strong as the woman sitting in my chair in that counseling session to tell me it would take five days to get over a man I'd talked to for a week or that I needed to see my psychiatrist *then*.

I had long stopped looking at emails from How About We, BabyBoomerPeopleMeet, Brainiac, EZmatchup, Chemistry, Match, BBWCupid, eHarmony, OkCupid, BBPeopleMeet, Nerve, SeniorPeopleMeet, Untrue and AmateurMatch as I bumped down the Zoloft stairs ten milligrams at a time, but as the Prozac began to take hold, first with its Technicolor dreams and then with a bit of its special gift of each morning being a new chance, I began to study dating.

One of the problems I found in my research is that one is thrown to the wolves with an information system at odds with itself. On the one hand there is so-called reality television, where average is okay, if you're a man, and on the other hand there is the Internet, which promises the perfect match for everyone. I've caterwauled about the fat people sites so I Googled other people VH1 and Bravo would reject and found sites for "cancer patients dating," "amputee dating," "burn victim dating," "gigolo dating," "Aryans dating," and "depressives dating."* Even "ferret owners dating" brought up a lively discussion on a general dating site.†

More magazine, which caters to the over-forty female, features dating advice from Patti Stanger, who sizes up the people who *pay* her with wince-inducing cruelty: "He's never been laid, has he?"‡ Among the dozen or so books devoted to the fifty-and-over set, one is faced with *Getting Naked Again*, which seems to me to jump the gun, or my gun, at least. My ambitions had dwindled to staying dressed, going to the new Woody Allen movie and he buys the popcorn, and working up to being on each other's speed dial. There is much advice for us oldsters on sex techniques, reviving that gung-ho teenaged enthusiasm and priceless but pointless factoids like, "More seniors are golfing today than ever before."§

---

* I had to laugh when I registered at nolongerlonely.com, a comprehensive "social community for adults with mental illness," and wondered how a dissociative would answer the questions of activity preference. In fact, the site caters to people with depression, eating disorders, autism/Asperger's, personality disorder, post-traumatic stress, anxiety, schizoaffective, bipolar, obsessive-compulsive and dissociative disorders. This puts a whole new spin on picking a favorite cuisine or movie genre . . .

† And, yes, there are "1000s of Sexy Midgets" waiting to find love online.

‡ *Millionaire Matchmaker*, Season 5: Ep. 3.

§ O'Brien, P. David, *Over 50 Dating Secrets*, Amazon Digital Services, 2012. Kindle edition.

Is any of this helpful? I wondered as I spent my birthday alone with Daisy, two dozen research essays, an Entenmann's something and a queue of Hulu *House* episodes. Don't twenty-five-year-olds need more advice on sex while women with back fat and lumpy veins need a Steve Ward to tell them what to talk about in a seventeen-floor elevator ride with single men whom they haven't been introduced to?

My father spends the winter in Arizona, so I headed off to the Land of Gated Communities for Christmas. That autumn he'd begun to keep regular company with Dot, the widow of one of his best friends. Dad and her deceased husband, Uncle John, were two of four med school lab partners who became a clique. Sharing a corpse for dissection can do that I guess. The other guys and their girls went to my parents' wedding and my mother was Dot's matron of honor when Dot married Uncle John.

I encouraged the little romance. I knew my mother would have loved seeing people she loved together, and it was Dot I sat down with and didn't leave at the little gathering in Sun City after my mother died. I didn't think of her as a surrogate mother but as someone fine and fragile and feminine, who already knew my parents had been married for sixty-five years.

When Dad and I went to her house for Christmas Eve my hopes of something more, er, *codified* were dashed. I knew from the number of photos of John in her living room that he was her one and only, despite the boyfriends she's had since he died. The white and gold Madonna pronounced her an old-timey Catholic, which would have made my father snort in derision. Thank God, sometimes, he's blind. Her home, in fact, was white and gold, spindly satinwood china cabinets full of pale Lladró, brocade Queen Anne chairs and chandeliers. It was lovely, but someone would have to put his or her personality in hiding if they lived together because my parents' house was leather club chairs and couches, Southwestern art and about two million CDs.

How would Dot react to one of Dad's experiments in Debussy? How would she react when he spilled spaghetti sauce on the carpet? How would he survive Fox News?

"By living in separate rooms, just like he and Mom did," my brother laughed when we talked on Christmas Day. Except that it was taste, not politics and religion, that kept my parents apart. Mother's addiction to *Wheel of Fortune* was a long way from Sean Hannity, and Hannity was a very, very, very old universe away from Stephen Hawking and *The Nation*.

My parents' marriage had its times of union and times of deep disconnect. Mother turned to the Vatican II Church like it was Heathcliff, but Dad lives on his own planet of books and music and a hundred interests and he can be indifferent where other people would be angry or hurt or sympathetic. Once, in Rome, when I was bleary-drunk, they jitterbugged to a Big Band orchestra and the dance floor cleared for them, they were that good, that synchronized. But then there was my mother, after her stroke, being admitted to a nursing home and screaming that she'd spent her life being Mrs. Kuffel and her name was Marie. She resented my father's intelligence and probably feared his sarcasm. She also refused a heart valve procedure that would have prolonged her life on the questionable "if" of its success. She was adamant. "I want to be here for my husband." My father was blind and she was tethered to oxygen and between them they were almost one healthy body.

Individually, however, I not only loved them, I liked them a lot. They were stoic, funny and strong. For three days in a row, a social worker asked my mother if she understood what going into hospice care meant. Mom couldn't remember the conversation from the day before but she understood the concept. "It means I'm dying." The social worker then repeated the question of how she felt about that and each day Mom said the same thing: "Shit happens."

Dad was listening to a book about Magellan's voyage to the Pacific while I made Christmas dinner for him, Dot and me. My mother's disinterest in his books-on-tape was such that he either would have put his earphones on or retired to their bedroom to listen. One nice thing about being alone with him was getting to hear the story of Magellan's death, the price Europeans would pay for the cloves and cinnamon I was using liberally, how the fleet hobbled home in one ship with eighteen of the original crew of 270.

I wouldn't mind being married to a man like Dad, I thought. He's curious, a fact-collector, prone to tangents ("Giggle—Google; whatever—sixteenth century Brunei, wouldja? Were they Moslems then?"), a foodie and a traveler. He even loves to shop. I thought about that afternoon five months later when I signed an over-the-top Father's Day card, "And that's why I never got married."

I haven't gotten married because I haven't met the right man who wants to marry me. But there may be some truth in the sentimental excesses that my brother must have rolled his eyes at while reading that card to Dad. Three thousand miles away, my father was still a great boyfriend because we are who we are to each other. He never put me to bed with a fairy tale when I was a kid, preferring to answer any questions I'd come up with lately. My questions tended to be about the atom bomb and cancer and how one dies from poisonous mushrooms, which made for some bad dreams but possibly also prevented me from being too much the little princess who sprouts into the beautiful bride. Maybe I dashed too far down Dad's road less taken and never learned the arts of girlishness with him, but he nourished my authenticity, my selfness.

Likewise, I was purely myself with my girlfriends, and in my sneaky bad-girl giggles with Kevin and Will. And if Will and Dad had known me all my life, I'd gotten close to Celia in chance meetings with our dogs at night, and meeting Bette or Jean and Ben had been like seeing parts of myself in a mirror for the first time. And each time I talked to Kevin, it was the first oh-my-God-where-have-you-been-all-my life feeling that bubbled up from deep in my belly. Intimacy, I thought as the three us sat down to roast duck and stuffed squash, is possible and as simple as nectar from a petunia, and it deepens with time. No fake cheerfulness, no denying the demon depression, no reason not to think I will be enjoyed.

*   *   *

As I thought about first meetings, I couldn't escape Dar, although he was the other living proof that deep understanding between two people can be terminated. I hadn't spoken to him in more than half a year, but I sent him one of the couple of dozen Christmas cards I managed to write between final essays and failing to wrap or send gifts to my family. He hadn't emailed me either, so I wondered if we were at a mutual impasse or if he was busy and trusting.

A wiser person would have skipped the card and not picked up the telephone.

"Frances! I was wondering when you'd call. How are you?"

"Okay. How are you?"

"You know. Busy. Statistics kicked my ass this semester. And everyone in the family is broke, so instead of giving presents we decided to paint one room in each of our houses for each other. I've been back and forth to Gilbert and Randolph and Fountain Hills with piles of drop cloths and all our gear. It's been crazy. When can I see you?"

I drummed my fingers on the kitchen table. His question was more about him than me. When could he find a break in his schedule?

"I could drive to Scottsdale," I said in a voice low enough not to betray tears. "Maybe we could have lunch."

"That would be great! I get off work tomorrow at two. How about a late lunch?" He gave me directions to a strip mall. I started to write them down and then quit. If I couldn't speak a few sentences without wanting to cry, there was a good chance I was going to have a whale of a stomachache tomorrow, much too ill to get more than twenty feet away from the bathroom.

"How's your dad?" he asked. "How's Daisy?"

"Dad is obsessed with Magellan and Daisy's with her Uncle Benedict and Auntie Jean, behaving much better than she does for me. How's your mother? How's Gulliver?"

"Mom's good. Gulliver has been naughty, though. Each time we're both out of the house, he goes into Mom's room and sleeps on her bed."

"You could shut the door."

"Mom used to do that but it's unsatisfying to me; I want a training solution." One of Dar's minimum-wage jobs before he found his philanthropic calling was training dogs. Gulliver can high-five, down-stay, and die very slowly. It was good to know the perfect Gulliver had a failing.

"Mom got him a bed for Christmas. He likes it—as long as I'm in the room with him. I don't know where he got the idea he could get up on the furniture."

"Wouldn't you, if you were a dog?" I asked. "I mean, a doggie bed is nice, but your mom's double bed is sweet."

"I have to figure this out."

"You should get a tiger to sleep on her bed when she's not home."

"Yes! That might do it! I've been scheming ways to booby trap the bed. Hadn't thought of a tiger."

"Or a shark. That would scare him off. As long as it doesn't cause a fishy smell in the house," I went on, considering. "I'm sure if you're consistent about bathing and brushing it each week, and taking it to the groomer to have its anal glands and toenails clipped, the shark won't smell too bad."

"A shark should do it."

"Glad I could help," I said. "I'll see you tomorrow at three?"

"I'm looking forward to it."

* * *

At two the next afternoon I wandered out of the guest bedroom in my pajamas to make a peanut butter sandwich.

"You better hurry if you're going to Scottsdale," my father said.

"I'm not going."

"What's with you and Dar these days? You don't talk about him much."

I sat down and turned off his four-track tape player. The monotone reader ceased his narration of the weakened Swiss banking industry. "I'm in love with Dar. He's not in love with me. I'm crawling out of this depression and I don't think it would be good for me to see him. I'm fat and sad and have nothing to say."

"Humph." He leaned forward to turn his magazine back on. "I never did see you and Dar together."

What did that mean? I could "see" Dad and Dot together—for a while. They were great old friends and enjoyed going to Sunday brunch or having dinner together, and they liked Glenn Miller and . . .

For a while.

Then I thought of Ruth, Dad's next-door neighbor. She was big and big-hearted, always bringing food over and inviting him to go to the pool with her. It was thank-Jesus-this and

Jesus-done-that and her cooking was terrible. I had forbid my father to take up with Ruth and he nearly gagged laughing.

I could not "see" him with Ruth. He could appreciate Ruth's kindness but she put his hackles up only a little less than she riled mine.

What did Dad "see" when Dar and I were together? The age difference? My weight? His self-containment? My moods? I was perplexed because in the big things like religion and politics, which I knew Dad and Dot had to bury, Dar and I agreed straight down the line. Dar was obsessed with *The Andy Griffith Show* and I could sometimes spend a day flaked out with whatever city's housewives happened to be on TV, but where our tastes were different, we could appreciate the other's sensibilities.

Or did he not sense a spark that's different from "getting" someone? How cruel if that was true. I mean, Dar and I could have parsley sex (a nice relish but not the meal) but what could Dot and Dad do with their chemistry? I knew for a fact that they weren't counting the hours until I left so they could get back to business.

Dar was in transit from Maryvale and I left a faint message of illness and regret on his cell phone and went back to bed and my Kindle and apricot jam on the pillowcase.

*   *   *

He called around five that afternoon. He was volunteering at an animal shelter the next day and going to a party that night but maybe I could drive over for breakfast the day after that? No, I said. That was my second day before leaving and I wanted to be available for Dad's last errands and tasks. He was quiet a moment and said, "I get that. You have an infinite number of breakfasts in your life but not many Christmases with your father left."

I was relieved. Enough that when he asked about the autumn I told him how grim it had been and then confessed, nearly in a whisper, "One reason I'm not frothing to see you is because I've gained so much weight."

"You know I don't care about that."

"But I do. It's been hard for me to be around people because of it."

He sighed. "I know how you feel. I need to lose some weight, too, but there's so little time to exercise."

I hate that response. The difference between a forty-year-old male needing to lose 40 pounds is not in the same ballpark as a fifty-three-year-old female needing to lose nearly 140 pounds. But I let it pass. "Don't they have a gym at the university?"

"Yeah, but, well, you know—"

He was busy. I think Dar was born busy. He probably came busting out of the womb with a Post-it note to paste on his mother's chest saying he'd be back for his next feeding but would be over at someone's house building a website or training a mastiff. I'd known him in the one un-busy spell in his life, when his apartment lease was up and he was waiting for a sublet in Florida where he planned to get straight, rethink his life and un-depress himself on the beach. When that failed and he found himself in hock to American Express, he headed home to his mother and promptly got busy again.

"You look fine," I told him. "You look the same as always in that Facebook picture."

"Maybe you're too hard on yourself with this weight and food plan thing, Frances."

My throat had a lump like Gibraltar in it. I always feel better when I'm abstinent. It should be an end unto itself. But with Dar, it was about my weight. So he could lose a few? He'd turned his life around in five years, was working on a master's degree and training abandoned pit bulls to be golden retrievers. I was living on an adjunct's pittance and random dog gigs, getting fatter. I desperately wanted to show him the other me—the thin, mountain-pounding me, the one that when I wasn't smiling didn't look like I was actually scowling from the fat pulling my mouth down, the one who rode the Cyclone at Coney Island ten times in a row, screaming with my nephew, just because I could finally fit. In a way, Dar had never met me.

I sniffed loudly. "I wish I was too hard on myself. If I was, I might get my ass into a 12-step room and find my ass fit the chair a lot better. I don't like not being able to do things."

"Yeah, that makes sense. You're on meds, though, right?"

"Prozac. I'm up to forty milligrams. I'm better, but I have a way to go."

"You're gonna be fine. Frances, I gotta take a shower. I'm driving some friends around the bars tonight."

"I have a Christmas present for you. I'll mail it." Last year I gave him a cotton candy machine, NIB from eBay, and he'd been as excited as I'd hoped he'd be.

That was before we'd gone to Santa Fe.

This year I got him a *Mayberry R.F.D.* cookbook. If I couldn't win his heart, I could harden his arteries.

"You shouldn't do that. Just let me know sooner when you're coming. I will always find time for you. That and your Christmas cards are our tradition."

"I'll mail it," I said again. I wanted to skip over the finding time thing. Until I was better—thinner, at peace, out of love—it was I who refused to give Dar the time to form any new opinions. "I'm glad you liked the card. It was a photo I took in Prague."

"I think my mom's gonna frame it, she loves it so much."

"Tell her thank you."

"I will. Have fun with the rest of your visit, okay?"

"'Bye," I whispered, and hung the phone up as gently as if it were an egg.

• • •

There were a few dozen emails after my failure to show myself at Christmas. Gulliver continued to get on his mother's bed and I suggested giving the shark a whip or a cattle prod, at which Dar cyber-snickered. "Be careful what you feed me," I wrote back to his laughter. "I can live very well on a steady diet of whimsy."

"Well, I want you to live very well, so I'll feed you a whimsy buffet if that's what it takes," he replied a few hours later. Why did we flirt when he didn't love me?

On Valentine's Day, always a horrid day for the single woman and, probably, most men, he emailed that Lady Antebellum, whose idiot song "Need You Now" we had searched the radio for across the high desert of New Mexico and Arizona, had done well at the Grammys.

"This really is the perfect Valentine's note." I remembered him scrolling through the dial searching for the anthem of friends with benefits. "And now I have enough information to look them up on YouTube. She looks *exactly* how I pictured her—like a post-modern Tennille, although not quite so toothy. I don't think this group knows what 'antebellum' means, do you? Because if they do, that means they're geniuses, singing Underground Railroad songs of love. Hope you get a big Whitman's sampler in a red velvet box," I ended.

Five hours later, after classes were over and he could check his texts, he wrote back, "What I love about you, aside from your ability to determine a woman's exact features through the radio, is your ability to capture the commercial essence of American Valentine's Day in a closing wish."

I made a joke in return as my glasses collected my tears. Email is fabulous for hiding behind jocularity, I decided. Later that day he came home and found the Christmas present I'd finally mailed off.

"I love the Aunt Bee cookbook! So awesome. I immediately shared it with my mom and she was pretty excited, too, and told me again her favorite trivia tidbit about Aunt Bee: 'You know, she died a pauper.' A postmodern, less toothy Tennille—heh. And carpetbaggers of love! I do enjoy your wit. And I wish you some fun."

He loved parts of me the way mammals love salt. These days I had no one to bring out the silly in me. We were at the sticking place.

These exchanges lasted a day or two and then lapsed for a month. In March, Dar asked me more about why I'm susceptible to the Black Dog and I wrote the kind of letter Ashley Wilkes probably wrote Melanie Hamilton on each anniversary of her death. "I would like to tell [my younger self] to truly believe in herself, to be happy with who she is. I'd tell her not to be afraid and I'd tell her what decent, respectful, basic treatment is and that she should kick anyone who didn't give her that. Being afraid and going along is the bane of my existence. I'd make up blind dates for her and I would hope she'd have a kid or two. I'd encourage her to save for old age. I wish she knew she was okay, that she didn't have to remain the mistake she was in utero. But I'm 54. It's too late."

"I'm going to save this in my inbox for periodic remindering," he enthused back. "I don't think it's all too late. When you're ninety, you'll feel the same about now as now you feel about your 20s. I'm pumped; let's do this stuff!"

It was too late for me. My confidence crumbles like heavy snow on a thin snowpack. There will be no kids for me. My old age will be one of poverty. The one thing I could feel proud of in that exchange was that I had offered my very best advice to him. I'd tried to be noble. And having tried, it was finally time to really end it.

I took the wimp's way out and lapsed into silence and deleted him from my Facebook friends. Six weeks later he blithely checked in on how the book was progressing and I sniped, "Have you found the mother of your children yet?" He responded with protests that he was not screening women for fertility and whatever else he wanted from an ideal mate, although, he admitted, "I did post briefly on OkCupid last summer and I have dated a girl I met through that (and she and her kids have recently enjoyed some homemade cotton candy, thanks to you)."

I thought I'd given everything I had to give him until I found out he was giving my stuff to other women. I felt ugly and pointless as a dying woman and the next day I told him it hurt too much to write him. He pled innocence—"Why would it be painful?" he asked all cyber-wide-eyed, and I replied crisply that perhaps he didn't notice that I hadn't initiated one in twenty email conversations in the last year and that I'd removed him from Facebook.

Facebook brought him up short. Somehow that convinced him I'd truly slunk off to curl up in the thick undergrowth of my psyche. With his own cyber-pain he wished me well and said good-bye.

•   •   •

It's been more than four months since that last dialogue. Peonies have given way to roses, which gave way to lilies, which were crushed in a hurricane. Indian summers seem to be a thing of the past in the age of global warning. The trees are dropping their leaves without changing color.

My heart hasn't died, but I will have to clean my glasses and have a cigarette after finishing this chapter. Dar's and my love ricocheted as failure but even in that we're partners. Of all the men I'd dated, talked to, emailed, winked at or otherwise brushed against in this year, Dar was the only one who loved me.

That's the strangest part of it. Dar cared about my work and dogs and sanguinity. It was a poison we both had to swallow in order for me to finally confront the despair that is at the root of my loneliness.

Eleven

There are moths that drink the tears of elephants.
Tears contain salt, water and trace levels of
protein. Mabra elephantophila steals the tears
without the elephants seeming to notice.
Lobocraspis griseifusa does not wait for an
animal's eyes to moisten—it sweeps its proboscis
across the eye of its host, irritating the eyeball,
encouraging it to produce tears.

I was back in bed in March, immobilized by fear after enrollment once again dropped and I lost my teaching job. I had some
small savings and pulled myself together enough to put the word
out that I was back in the dog business. Slowly, gigs began to
sprout up.

Ten months earlier, I'd promised myself no more pinched
nerves from suddenly beagle-hating Labs. Now it was a Portu-
guese water dog that flipped out as humans suddenly spurted
forked tails and horns. Daisy was amused and treated him like
a windup toy. One growl from her and the whole pedestrian
population turned into Hieronymus Bosch's *Death of the Rep-
robate*.

A French bulldog, dachshund, Boston terrier and elderly golden retriever joined my roster. I began to breathe again. They couldn't pull my arms from their sockets and, by coaching a couple of writers, I was making the same wages I'd made adjuncting.

Plus, no papers to mark and no students to argue about plagiarism with.

I walked the streets that slowly came to life after a brutal winter, enumerating to Eva, the Frenchie, the things I had to do in order to fully pull out of my depression and explaining to Trixie, my rickety dachshund, about how to write a book about volunteering to go out and get hurt by a bunch of weird guys.

Because getting hurt, I came to understand, is the norm in dating. It's pain I need to steer clear of.

• • •

With that in mind, I decided to go back to craigslist, where I would get some immediate attention for the specifics I was looking for.

I was not especially looking for a boyfriend, but I wanted to flirt. What I wanted was experience and information and some fun. I proposed a dim sum Chinatown date for research purposes—I've never had dim sum, Chinatown is my favorite neighborhood, and research would take the onus off the boy-girl-chemistry-weight-competition-looks-dog-hair thing that had caused so many pinches the summer before.

* * *

I was late and I could tell Jacob was not pleased. He'd driven in from Connecticut, it was his birthday, his sixty-second, and the woman he was meeting for the first time hadn't bothered to charge her cell phone before trying to find a train on a Saturday night.

But he was cute, in an impish sort of way, and we were meeting in Washington Square, which is entertaining, and I was wearing a shortish skirt and feeling flirty.

We had dinner at a macrobiotic restaurant and my shoes gave me blisters. I bought bandages and he offered to rub my feet but I was too embarrassed to accept. What would I owe him for a public foot rub?

He drove me home and we found him a strong cup of coffee sold by a cute kid to whom he spoke Hebrew. It turned out that Jacob had fought in the Six-Day War. I mulled that over as we walked to the Promenade. Any man Jacob's age would have had to come to terms with war, whether because he was in one or had found a way around it. Something about the way he informed me of his Israeli army service hinted at a dark side of his soul. I assumed that he didn't have to join the Israeli army and by doing so was ditching the American draft my brothers went to Vietnam under. Eager to contribute to my research, he told me that the last woman he'd dated had lost her job and moved in with him after an invitation to stay for a couple of days. He described renovating his house and the features of his SUV and I liked his attention to comfort but had visions of

Daisy running in with muddy paws and jumping on the white couches.

I emailed my thanks for dinner and the chat and he responded and friended* me on Facebook.

We remain Facebook contacts but I wouldn't say we became friends.

* * *

Joe looked like a good prospect. He said he knew some good dim sum places and we began to work out the details for meeting. In the middle of that, instant messenger popped up.

"Someone's co-opted your address," Paul wrote. "I keep getting offers of Russian brides from you. You need to change your password."

I responded with a chuckling emoticon and promised I'd take care of it. On the other hand, I wondered, didn't the former Soviet Republics still have a lot of Jews? Maybe he should consider Russia his land of opportunity. American citizenship in exchange for a wig? Not bad, really.

"How are you?" he replied

"Good," I said. "Did you find your summer girlfriend last year?"

He answered, ":(."

"Maybe you should try JDate."

---

* It is time for spell check to accept "friend" as a verb.

"I have. I didn't find anyone and the fees are enough to have a good dinner at Vegetarian Ginger."

I thought about putting him in touch with Jacob. They might each know a girl for the other.

. . .

One night, I was walking Daisy and her pal, Honey Bear, and we passed a bike I'd admired earlier that day. The rim of one slim tire was red, the other yellow. The frame of the bike was robin's egg blue, the grips on the bullhorn handlebars were emerald green, and the seat was black-and-white racing checks. As bicycles go, it was a piece of art.

As I waited for Daisy to pee, a tall skinny kid came tripping down the stairs of the apartment building the bike was locked up to. Daisy finished and I waited again for Honey Bear to circle around and pee over Daisy's piddle.

"Whoa! Check it out," the kid said. "Will the yellow one have to start it over again?"

I laughed. "No. Daisy's usually too confident to cosign, but sometimes I have a couple of other dogs who line up behind her. They don't do it for each other. Only Daisy."

"Alpha bitch," he said soothingly, holding out his hand. Daisy jumped on him, clipping his groin, and washed her tongue across his face.

"She's very European and she likes you, which you should take as a compliment. I don't believe in alpha dogs. When Daisy wrestles it's always on her back. A vicious dog could rip her guts out. I have several theories about pee-overs but dominance isn't one of them."

He walked over to the bike and began unlocking it. "What's the other dog? It's some kind of crazy."

"Chow and Australian shepherd, we think. She's very nice. Your bike is amazing, by the way."

"You grock it, huh?" I blinked. I haven't used or heard the word "grock" in maybe forty years. Since the time I had a skateboard, in fact.

"Totally."

We began to walk along Clark Street, the kid asking questions about the dogs. He told me he went to St. Ann's, the neighborhood's elite and very progressive prep school, and that he was not doing well academically. That means, in Annese, he's too busy making claymation videos to music he composes himself to take Latin as seriously as his teacher would like. They don't give grades at St. Ann's but he'd probably ace his SATs in the first go and end up majoring in physics and film studies at Stanford.

He was the kind of kid I should have dated back in the days of grocking on crude skateboards, the source of the kind of regrets I have about weighing 245 pounds when this dating stuff and general confidence got worked out and you went to the prom in an evening gown from the '50s and couldn't wait to begin your freshman year at Reed College . . .

It was a testament to how much better I was feeling that I could appreciate this chance meeting rather than spiraling into milk long spilt and long soured.

He stopped in front of the Korean deli and asked if I'd watch his bike for a minute. "I know the guy inside. He'll accept my ID."

"How old are you?"

"Sixteen."

"What are you going to do tonight?" I asked.

"Hang out with my friend back where we met. I live on Garden Place. I'll go home around one."

At sixteen, Will and I spent most of our weekends drunk on the pretty good wine my father made—and we could *drive*. What the hell, I thought. Rites of passage shouldn't force you to lie. "How about if you hold the dogs and I go buy your beer?"

He thanked me profusely when I handed him the plastic bag and told me where I could toss over a thousand bucks for a bike like his and rode off as the dogs and I continued toward Cadman Plaza.

Kids, I justified to myself, are kids—better beer than getting into either kid's parents' Stoli.

I had to call Will when I got home. We'd spent those years together—or together in our apartness as two weird teenagers, one fat, the other gay, who tried to find something other than each other to belong to. "Wouldn't you have done it?"

"Of course. Why should we have gotten to have all the fun? They have five more years before they're legal. We were always just a couple of years away from eighteen. Can you imagine what we'd have done without your father's wine cellar, France?" Will grew up poor as a rock and my parents kept me on a fairly short allowance. We would have been scared, broke and bored, although Will might have come out earlier than high school graduation, bored into bed with some college student.

"I can't drink red wine anymore," I said. "It makes my ankles blow up."

"We're old," he said sadly. Lately every conversation comes down to our decrepitude and neuroses. "Thank God I have Rico. How's Daisy?"

I get that a lot from my family. They mention a mate or child or friend and then ask how Daisy is. The difference between them and Will is that he prefers the company of dogs as well.

"Her muzzle turned white this summer. And the tip of her tail." My voice sank. It was hard, seeing her getting older.

"She's eight. She has a long time still. But, France, how did she get to be eight? And when are you going to get another dog? You're not getting any younger, you know."

"You can only say that because you still have a week of being fifty-three."

He giggled his giggle that always drags me down with him. "You know what I'm doing on my birthday?" he whispered.

"No. What?"

"*Golfing.*"

Over 50 Dating Secrets reared its hoary head in triumph. "Oh, God, we *are* old. Can I come live with you when we're supposed to retire only I don't have any retirement? I'll teach your puppies not to eat linoleum."

"I want cabana boys."

"I don't mind cabana boys."

"We'd make a good old married couple," he said. "I'll watch cabana boys I can't get it up for and you'll watch Book TV about stuff you can't remember."

"It's a deal."

· · ·

I knew competition was a factor with Joe when it became difficult to find a time to meet. I may lack dim sum experience but am fairly certain it's a brunchy thing, not a Friday night thing. On Saturday morning, though, he had a fiction-writing workshop, and he was meeting friends on Sunday.

"God, help me," I said to my computer screen. Men in their fifties who take fiction workshops are, I'm afraid, doomed to being perpetual wannabes.

I liked the good hard dry kiss Joe gave me when we met and his fairly good-natured realization that we weren't going to find one of those palaces trafficked by rolling steam tables. We found dumplings on a menu and he dove in with enjoyment until I told him the beer story.

"I can see how it's funny," he said, putting his chopsticks down, "but as the father of teenagers . . ."

Is this also a component of regret? In missing parenthood, was I barred from having my stomach clutch at the dangers my seed faces?

"I remember a New Year's Eve party I had in high school. I was shocked when my mother came into the living room and poured vodka into the punch bowl. 'I'd rather you drink what's here and that you drink it openly. It will make you drink like adults.' She was wise about that."

"I dunno," he said.

I can't tell you what we talked about by the time the last of the scallion pancakes was gone. I probably tried to be interested in his novel and he probably tried to be interested in women and weight issues. We walked down Mulberry Street and he seemed oblivious to the St. Anthony Giovinazzo street fair. He treated the oompah-band and cheap pastel plush toy prizes, the blocks of torrone and ropes of peppers, the divine smell of sausages and hot grease for zeppole as a nuisance because of the crowds. Had I been alone with my camera, it would have been a pageant. But I was accommodating. If he wanted to move quickly through it, I'd dart behind the booths and snake against the crowds eager to shoot balloons and grab a deep-fried Oreo.

I was, therefore, surprised when he insisted on getting off the train and walking dogs with me. We walked him back to the R train and he said, "This was fun. We should probably do it again."

I gave him the same hard dry kiss he'd greeted me with and agreed.

If the conversation was diffident, we at least both liked to read. He was handsome. And I never heard from him again.

•   •   •

Here's another piece of dating etiquette I'd like everyone to play along with: Don't say "we'll do it again" unless you mean it.

Let's all agree on a polite "It was nice meeting you" as a way of leaving the door unlocked but quite closed.

And this is where perspective comes in.

Joe's—let's call it rudeness, shall we?—pinched me. I'd rushed headlong into Galean and Jeremy and their rejections hurt like hell at a time when my reserves were at low ebb. It took days to put the individuals, if not the defeat, behind me.

Pain, however, is months of the Black Dog sitting on my chest. It's financial precariousness that feels like rejection even though I know that enrollment numbers are behind it and the pay wasn't great to begin with. Pain is going out during an ice storm at night for cake, pain is missing my mother and pain is what I feel in the midst of a silent quarrel with Bette.

Hurt is finite. Pain is static. It hangs around. When it becomes less acute, it leaves you with a hangover. It is the difference between a skinned knee and a torn ligament. You'll walk again. You'll go sightseeing and make Thanksgiving dinner and go shopping for the perfect evening gown. But you will never have the nerve to try a Salchow again.

There is an ad on Facebook right now that vacillates from "I ❦ Being Single" to "I ♡ Being Single." The semantics here are bizarre. First of all, why does this "brand spanking new on-line dating site/unique events" switch back and forth between love and something-other-than-love? The two hearts suggest that the service caters to both kinds of client, but its motto, "Don't Ride Alone," is definitely relationship-centric.

Beyond this wide cast of the net for clients, the symbols themselves are strange. Is the first jagged heart a broken heart or a half a heart? I can understand being brokenhearted after a romantic catastrophe, but anyone in a state of perpetual mourning because she or he is single is not my idea of an ideal date. It brings me back to the philosophy stuffed constantly down our single throats by the dating, beauty, diet, marriage and entertainment industries: If the sign means halfhearted, is a singleton half a person? Either statement suggests that meaning comes through romance, rather than through the affirming or negating actions of how one actually gets through one's days.

I've broken my heart a couple of times and the duration of the wound is the double-pain of the loss of the man and of never spinning over ice again. I'm not brokenhearted because I'm single. There are moments of acute hurt in being single, a cold ache of being an outsider and loneliness. It hurts, sometimes a lot, and then passes. I laughed when a couple smooched loudly enough on the street that it made Daisy bark, and I wished Joe would wander off to browse at Housing Works while I watched the girl too chubby for her low-riders and tube top jumping for joy when her boyfriend won a pink teddy bear.

Dar, who lurks behind these words, causes, at the worst of times, a cascade of feelings: dismay, anger, curiosity, well-wishing, loss of hope, regret, self-judgment, silence, need, boredom. Each has its own spasm. I wonder if he's fallen in love. I wish he could read the novel I'm working on. I need a good laugh. I hope he finds the perfect job and starts rock climbing again.

I hope, if he thinks of me, that he misses something he hasn't quite found with anyone else. I hope I've left some hole in him—but I hope it only hurts a little.

I want badly to text "I miss you" to Dar. A lot of what hurts is my pride. Then I read about the Wall Street protests or chat with Celia about her work in Albany and I forget again for a while.

It's a good thing that Dar and I didn't see each other more than once or twice a year. It's a good thing to keep pain and hurt as separate categories in my head.

●　●　●

In a city whose restaurants are known for pressed tin ceilings, oak floors and enviable furnishing and décor, Abigael's on Broadway is the spitting image of the convention rooms at the Hunt Valley, Maryland, Marriott.

I had never seen a heterosexual man enjoy a duded-up strawberry margarita as much as Paul. The drink seemed bigger than him.

I dropped something on the medallion-patterned carpet and the woman at the table next to me made a joke about pocketbooks. I was relieved that she spoke to me, let alone found a female common denominator between us. Every woman in the restaurant wore hose, a wig, and a turtleneck. To my very slight credit, I had turned back to my closet and pulled out a blazer rather than the more comfortable shruggie. But with my bare legs, neckline, sandals and pierced ears, I could have been considered an insult to every person in the room.

I had started having afternoon coffees with Paul somewhere among the craigslist dates.

"The basic question," he said in his flat voice, "we use in judging gentiles is whether you observe the Noachide Laws. Murder, robbery, blasphemy, idolatry, eating flesh from a living animal, having courts of law, sexual immorality."

"Deal breaker," I said, refolding my napkin. "As a Montanan, I like my meat to scream when I cut into it." He studies my poker face, then laughs. "Most of those are what Catholics call mortal sins, except for idolatry—we do like our Michaelangelos and Berninis—and courts of law, which caused the Reformation in several European countries. But everything I've read says kosher sex is married sex. Won't you have to—I don't know. You don't have confession or penance, do you? Isn't having sex with me breaking the immorality law?"

"Wellll," he drawled. "We can't have kosher sex."

"So if it's not kosher it's not sex?" I shook my head. "What is it then, some form of masturbation?"

"No. Masturbation is forbidden."

"Is this like Catholic loopholes around marriage? If you aren't married in the Church then you can't be a divorcée in the Church either?" I couldn't shake the sense that dating a gentile would be a less-than proposition for the woman.

For me.

It was putting the cart in front of the horse, however. It took hard work to talk to Paul. We had nothing in common.

But those noontime coffees made putting on a skirt and coloring my hair a pleasurable break in my routine of dogs. They reminded me there was a *me*. A mingler, if you will, and girlie—or at least wistful of lost girliness.

. . .

"How was Shavuot?" I asked the next time we met. "Are you exhausted?"

"I spent it on the Upper East Side," he said, "going from synagogue to synagogue."

"Yes, but *how* was it?" I pressed. "Did you enjoy it? Did you have some new insight?"

"It was hot. I took refuge in the penguin house at Central Park Zoo."

That is when I knew I would clean the Bat Cave and ask him over. I was enchanted by the thought of this slight man in his over-large suit and fedora, blinking back the lights of sleeplessness and Leviticus, sitting in the cool dark tunnel watching the penguins gawk at him through the windows as they zoomed through their icy aquarium.

. . .

We didn't speak of emotional matters. Paul lives several worlds away, not only in one in which the year is tied to moons and ancient remembrances, but in a world of numbers and symbols. To his credit, he made his decision to get his doctorate in logic because one of the professors was a gorgeous blonde, but he didn't live in my world of shades of early summer foliage and grapefruit-scented bubble baths. If I asked him what love felt like, he'd probably say tolerance to the sixth power.

Did I mention I once had a huge crush on Mr. Spock?

· · ·

Emotions, desire, fantasies were email fodder. "I think we will have a love affair rather than an affair," he emailed after I pulled that description of Shavuot out of him. His eyes had lit up when I began laughing about the penguins. He knew he'd touched something in me, and it was probably the first time he saw my eyes light up as well.

· · ·

And then it was July and his kids were at their Chabad-Lubavitcher camp and he'd come back from visiting them in the Catskills on the Sunday of the Fourth of July weekend to have his birthday dinner with me. In his loose suit and fedora, trying to sip the foot-long glass of silly margarita, he looked like a kid's idea of dressing up in the Clark Kent costume.

I finished my salmon and he finished his smoked beef ribs and the chocolate-dipped strawberry from his drink and we headed for the Seventh Avenue train. I had bottled water in the refrigerator and plastic cups at home. He had a bottle of kosher white zinfandel in his backpack. He also, at my request, brought a pair of pajamas and his tefillin. This was not kinkiness. I was inviting him to sleep over and announcing myself as his summer shiksa.

"Why did the other men remove their hats and just wear their yarmulkes?" I asked as we walked through the warm night.

"I didn't think about it," he said. "I could have taken mine off as well."

"I felt like a harlot. I'm sorry for the way I dressed."

He stopped and looked intently at me. "I appreciated the cleavage," he said. I may have been the naughtiest thing he's ever done, being a plunging neckline in the fanciest kosher restaurant in New York. "Do you mind if I say that I like your rack?"

I laughed. "No, but it makes me feel like Bullwinkle."

He shook his hand. "Got nuttin' up my sleeve," he said in the goofiest voice I'd heard from him yet. I laughed; it reminded me that he'd grown up in a world closer to my own, eating hot dogs and playing baseball on Saturdays. This sudden solidarity made me want to link arms with him but, despite email confessions of wanting to kiss me on the Promenade or hold hands over coffee, any kind of public touching felt wrong.

We climbed into bed and he tolerated Daisy's adoration very well as we watched a movie. She retreated to be closer to the air conditioner and we made out. I had warned him that I needed to go slowly and he made it to second base before I withdrew. He lost his yarmulke and we had to turn on the light and disembowel part of the bed, which brought Daisy to the cozy space that we probably hadn't intended to have between us. I woke up long enough in the morning to see him swaying through his prayers. It was comforting, that drowsy moment of knowing he was wrapped up in tefellin and thanks while I dropped off to sleep some more. It was comforting to fold his pajamas later in the morning and put them in a drawer.

• • •

I wanted to know what my co-single women were like, so I registered as "Ludovico" on VenusDiva. My first thoughts were that they looked better for their age than I did, happier and dewier, and that they were a lot more articulate and interesting than the men. "The guy I'm looking for: He will have the brains of Albert Einstein, looks of Sam Elliott, sex drive of Bill Clinton, humor of Mel Brooks and the compassion of Ghandi [sic], so if you're not all that, just a nice guy would be perfect," read one post by a blonde bombshell who had me laughing and reconsidering either my profile or my gender preference.

On the other hand, there was damage and defiance in the postings that I'd never seen in men's descriptions. "I am tired of all the head games, and I refuse to play them," wrote one, and, "If you just want to play games, get a hooker or an Xbox, but just leave the rest of us alone. People's feelings are at stake here, so don't be rude." This was a plus-size site, but other women were as diffident about their size as I was. "My weight fluctuates in cycles. Looking for someone who will be interested in me regardless of where we are on the spectrum." I sympathized, imagining the same twenty or forty pounds from Thanksgiving to Easter and from Memorial Day to Halloween.

"No!" I wanted to shout at another attractive blonde who wrote, "I am a Disney Cinderella collector and do believe in dreams coming true." She was my age and ever-single. Maybe she ought to reconsider her baby blue and white fantasies. I doubt any single man wants those expectations in a first email nod.

Reading so many profiles was, in the end, depressing. Everyone loves nature, loves red wine and hanging out at home, loves the Yankees (or the Giants or golfing), loves to travel, loves animals, loves jazz, loves to cook, loves to laugh, loves to use the word "love" in such force that it is meaningless. Why not just slosh all the names into a hat and ascribe love by lottery? Everyone loves the same stuff so what's the difference?

The difference, I suppose, is penguins on a hot day.

·   ·   ·

It wasn't much of a pinch when, in mid-August, his kids back from camp, Paul emailed to ask if I would return his pajamas. One night a week for five weeks, we fooled around but did not actually have sex. Frankly, I didn't want to. Someone must have used the expression "sucking face" at a crucial moment in his sexual awakening because he nearly Hoovered my lips off my face.

I didn't have the courage to set up a charm school for him. I didn't want to hurt his feelings and I knew we wouldn't make it to the High Holidays that were fast on the heels of my return from my first visit to my hometown in Montana in eight years.

I was a little sad, though, when he handed me my apartment key.

Then again, there's always next summer.

. . . .

Or not.

I shared some steamy emails with the man who identified himself as Rhett Butler, but I was up to my eyeballs in dogs and writing deadlines. I came off as earthy and frank but not quite in the mood. I could have liked him but he was married. If a man is stuck in a sexless marriage, I decided, he either had to work it out or make the kind of arrangements Jeremy did. "Just about the only thing you could do," I emailed, "would be to sweep me away. I say that because I am *tired*—of dogs, my apartment, my neighborhood. Take me to Gettysburg or Salem or Cape May or to an ultra mod hotel in midtown. But I refuse to clean my apartment beyond what is reasonable—which is to say, not very—in order to stay in my apartment and do things I've done before. I want fresh air."

It seems as fair a statement as I can think of what I want.

Besides, Kevin—now working part-time in a salon and taking care of Grace's mother-in-law, who was declining with senile dementia—was facing his own depression that winter. He, too, knew what it was like to do the same thing day after day. Just as I walk the same dogs on the same routes, he tells Lily that *Wheel of Fortune* isn't on for another eight hours and that their house doesn't face Pennsylvania across Elliott Bay.

"What do you want?" I asked him in one of our morning check-ins.

"I want a life!"

"Get in line. But what is your life?"

Without pausing, he answered, "A small house with an acre of land where we can grow tomatoes and have chickens."

We? I was flabbergasted. I had begun applying for real jobs, to teach creative writing in universities. It would be good karma, I had decided, to send my CV to a university an hour from where Will teaches in Illinois.

He is, after all, family, and he had texted back, "I'm excited!"

I wasn't prepared to make a choice between them and there wouldn't be one if I got hired in Dust Mote, Kentucky. If I didn't get hired, though, I thought to myself, Seattle is where I've wanted to be for years. And if Kevin hadn't mispronounced himself, he was offering me not near but *with*. I have never done *with*.

"Have you thought about angora bunnies?" I asked. "My grand-niece in Oregon has one and makes good money selling the fiber."

"Bunnies?" Kevin squeaked in his googly voice. "I had an angora bunny when I was a kid. Her name was Princess."

*   *   *

Later in the week, I emailed him about the real life he wanted to create for himself, not the joke, encouraging him to use his imagination in doing this. Sarah, Lily's daugther and Grace's girlfriend, promised to buy him a house when Lily gets to the point of non-recognition: "Where do you want to live? What kind of travel do you want to plan? What kind of salon do you want to work in?"

"I'm a homebody," he emailed back. "I want bunnies and chickens and you and tomatoes and blackberry jam."

My throat closed up at that. He wanted me. I blew my nose and wrote back, "I gotta tell you, I don't like columbines. I think they look like wax."

"No shit," he responded.

"But hollyhocks," I typed, "are necessary."

I clicked send and waited, watery merriment dancing in my heart.

Twelve

Squids cuddle after they mate, but the females are stuck holding the semen in a pocket next to their mouths.

In April, Kevin is diagnosed with prostate cancer. He's scared not only of the extent of the cancer and of the surgery, but worried about how Lily will be taken care of in the days of weakness and tiredness that will follow him home from the hospital.

Thinking back on the cast of Winnie the Pooh, I find a plush kangaroo and send it to him without signing my name. I could hear his screams from three thousand miles away. Grace texts me a photo of him asleep in the hospital bed with the toy tucked securely next to him, the joey tucked securely in its mama's pouch. That photo kind of says everything about why I cry from the knowledge that I am his friend.

His recovery is tough and, in some ways, hindered by Grace's and Sarah's questions about how we will make a living on an acre of land. I can board dogs and Kevin can cut hair, but we'll need more income than that and I don't know whether I'll find adjunct work in Seattle. One evening I do something I have never done before: I do a cost analysis of raising angora rabbits, a rough exercise that shows we could make a few thousand dollars our first year out. If Kevin builds the hutches and if we breed and sell the rabbits, we could see more income yet. I send it to him, along with a photo of a German angora. Sarah and Grace are impressed and delighted by the rabbit that, in full hair growth, is the size and looks of a Malamute. For some reason, the photo and my financials convince them we'll do enough of enough things to get by.

* * *

Slowly, we begin to expand our future beyond bunnies. Kevin has fallen in love with the Noritake Azalea china set of which I have my grandmother's tea set* and a few random pieces I've bought from eBay and stowed away in the nether regions of my limited storage space.

One day in May he emails me the confirmation of winning six azalea dinner plates on eBay. "I've been orgasming over it ever since I saw it. We need the entire set."

I pull my kitchen apart and unwrap everything I've col-

---

* Currently residing with my niece in Oregon, along with some other china and furniture. The rest of my junk is in Montana. And you wonder why I feel so scattered all the time?

lected. There are dinner plates, saucers without cups (why?), a butter tub, salad plates, serving pieces. I photograph them and mince off to UPS to ship two enormous boxes to him.

By then we've gotten serious. He has decided we need settings for sixteen. I've bought books and learned that the china was sold as a premium from Larkin, a catalogue company that sold soap, toiletries and luxury potables. It was second only to Sears and with an order of, say, ten dollars, the customer could also buy furniture, china, clothing and other items that gave the American home what was called, from the 1890s to the 1930s, the "Larkin Look." Frank Lloyd Wright designed its headquarters in Buffalo, New York. One of Larkin's most popular premiums was the Noritake Azalea china and in the effort to keep selling it after each housewife had her basic dinner set, Noritake kept adding the most orgasm-worthy side pieces that speak to the different time that is in Kevin's and my hearts. Butter tubs. Whipped cream bowls. Comports. Cream soup *and* bouillon cups.

My father's parents were hit hard in the Depression. There were times the family of five lived on my father's paper route earnings. I imagine that my grandmother must have bought her set of teacups and saucers, salad plates, teapot and cream and sugar a piece at a time when she ordered soap and shirts. My mother gave me the set when I was in my twenties, warning me that although I had loved it since I was a kid, it was nothing special.

You can "buy it now" a square luncheon plate for $992 on eBay. We had our own *Antiques Roadshow* prize and didn't even know it.

Kevin and I know it now. "Holy shit," he wrote four or five months after I saw him in Seattle. "You should see my Discover Card bill."

I don't tell him that I've maxed out my Paypal Visa. It was already near the limit. I bought the syrup jug with under plate as a reward for walking a colleague's dogs for a couple of days in the high 90s. By buying a loop-handled relish dish, jam pot and cruet from one seller I have saved a bundle in shipping charges, I write him, leaving out the fact that several of those pieces are rare, which pretty much voids the savings in shipping.

You can see how this is going.

We're addicts, Kevin and I. He lives with an eighty-two-year-old woman whose frontal lobe is shriveling and he can't get an erection. I have no chair in which I can retire with *Anna Karenina* and a brain that is hounded by failures, unloveability, deficiencies.

But we have our china obsession. It is a statement of our future and our trust in each other. Piece by piece, we are working our way toward a service for sixteen. Sometimes the idea of living together seems as fragile as the compote dishes that cost way more than I can afford. Then I compare this friendship to the men I've loved or wanted to love and I'm astonished. Kevin and I aren't chasing ghosts. We're not looking for an ideal other but for our better selves and we have the great good luck to trick some of that betterness out in each other.

One day, after he texts me pictures of his blooming deck garden, I email him a link to a website with recipes that use flowers. He ponders the information and, a few days later, emails me that he's made a batch of lavender Johnny-jump-up jelly with a whiff of spearmint to jazz it up. A few weeks later he sends me an article about a local food truck that serves hamburgers with onion jam.

"Ooooh," I write back. "Onion and blackberry jam. With bacon!"

Soon enough, he texts me a picture of a dozen jars of deep purple blackberry jam that could change the face of pancakes forever.

And he's researched Long Island ducks and finds they walk upright and forage for food rather than dabbling. They don't depend on a pond. The eggs are prized and each duck lays about two hundred a year with no burning desire to brood. Even more fun, they imprint upon humans, so we could actually take them for walks!

"Here, à l'Orange! Here, Peking! How 'bout those Mariners, Pressed?"

I decide that for every day I stick to my food plan I'll throw a dollar in an oatmeal box so that we have a little working principle when the time comes, a ritual Kevin calls A Buck for A Duck. I save catalogues and cut out pictures of chickens and Labradors, wicker lawn furniture and drying lavender, punctuated by sayings like "Sometimes I laugh so hard tears run down my leg," which, post-menopause and post-prostate, is a joke we both live with. Give me a collection of magazines and catalogues, an interesting box, glue and Mod Podge, and I can be happily obsessed for several days.

• • •

We are *playing*, long distance. I haven't known how to play since I was fourteen years old and my nieces co-opted my Barbie dolls.

By December we've amassed most of our service for sixteen and Kevin has sent me boxes of jellies and jams no one has imagined before.* I send an email to my dog clients and, after they bought out my supply, a check for $600 to Kevin by Christmas. We've added another teeny rivulet of income to the farmette.

There is no schedule for senile dementia, however, and no straight, predictable path for how the disease expresses itself. In Lily's case, it is with paranoia whenever Kevin speaks on the phone. As her ability to do simple tasks or be alone erodes, he is pretty much tied to her for all but three six-hour stints a week when a caregiver takes over. He uses the time for AA meetings and step work, haircuts and running errands for Grace and Sarah.

We speak less and less often. His mood is angry and rebellious that winter; mine ping-pongs between depression and extreme anxiety. It's easy to see why Kevin is in such a foul place: He fights insomnia only to wake to the sound of footsteps

---

* Caramelized onion bacon blackberry jam; blueberry mint ginger jelly; papaya peach bacon jam; apple bacon butter; lavender Johnny-jump-up jelly; strawberry ginger pineapple jam; pumpkin toasted pecan butter; blackberry rosemary jam; pumpkin pear toasted almond butter.

when Lily gets up to wander the night. He's in charge 150 out
of 168 hours a week.

My own depression is unfocused but one night, I gather my
medications before bed and find myself holding the bottle of
Klonopin and looking at it consideringly. I had not, that night,
felt as terrible as usual, which is, perhaps, why I could contem-
plate the bottle with such cold neutrality. I am as transfixed as
a kid seeing fireworks for the first time and when I snap to with
it in hand, I quickly put it back on the shelf, take my pills, turn
out the light and leap into bed with the Black Dog of despair
on my chest.

I despair because I can't die. Daisy would be bereft, at least
for a while. I would be leaving too much debt and too much stuff
for my family to sort out. My father is ninety-five. I couldn't do
that to him. I want out but am tied down. I can't imagine my
future, want and wish for nothing. The Bat Cave feels like a tomb.

But there are things I can do, I realize a few days later. My
VHS player doesn't work and I can get rid of all those movies.
If I were ever a size 8 or 18 again, those clothes belong to a
different Frances—a more successful one, maybe, or perhaps
one who defined herself by the clothes she owned. My nieces
are thrilled to get streams of emails with photos of the smallest
sizes and once a week I haul boxes to UPS or to Housing Works
for donation. Salvation Army comes and takes five enormous
bags away. I partner up with one of my Friends of Daisy, Jane,
and start posting both our clothes on eBay. I luck into an ongoing freelance editing gig that allows me to start really paying
credit cards down.

I am obsessed with stripping down my life, crumbling my debt. Dad and Daisy can have all the time they need because I want to be free.

The farmette hasn't disappeared from my future but Kevin has largely disappeared from my present. The game of collecting dishes from a year ago is over. I have no more jam to sell.

"I was suicidal a couple of weeks ago," I tell him in one of our few phone calls. He is in his car with fifteen minutes on Lily's caregiver's clock.

"I saw your blog," he says. "I didn't know what to say."

I brush his response out of the conversation immediately, asking about Lily, his roster of haircuts, Sarah and Grace's travel plans. It takes a couple of days for me to grow angry that he read the Klonopin story and didn't call me, even if he had to wait for Lily to go to bed and it was one in the morning in New York.

Did he care?

I don't know. I still don't know. A former drinking buddy of his dies in the spring and his response is that he's so sorry he hadn't had time to make his amends. He tells me more of the story later and sighs. "He died and I didn't. It's so weird, Frances. If he'd gotten sober, maybe . . . You know," his voices changes from sad to final, "this program really works. The more thorough I am about my shortcomings, the more peace I have. I'm more patient with Sarah and Grace, more grateful that they can afford to go out and have such good times. I have to stay upbeat and positive for Lily and I can do that. I don't want to have regrets about my attitude when she doesn't know me anymore."

I murmur appropriate things but I am in no sympathy with contentment, largesse, gratitude, love.

After the call, I text Will that I think I should come visit him. He writes back that he's on his way to Hong Kong for a conference. After he returns, I tell him I'm free in July but he never does set a date. When does life happen? Do we have to wait until Step Nine? Do we wait until Lily is babbling in diapers? Would ECT shake me out of my clenching agoraphobia, my chains to Debt, Dad and Daisy? Is one night in Chicago an infringement?

My psychiatrist increases my antidepressant dosage but only after making an appointment with her has been a note on my desk for two weeks.

I tell Jane some of this as we photograph our barely worn Eileen Fishers and Dana Buchmans.

"I think you should cut Kevin a break," she says.

"Why? Is it so hard to pick up the phone and say, 'Boy, you sound like you're in a really painful place. I feel for you'? He could have emailed that and it would have been a glimmer of hope for me."

"Men aren't good at this sort of thing." She holds up her hand to stop me. "Even gay men. I'm pretty good at it, though. Come to me. Go to Jean. Call your therapist—I'm sure she'd rather talk to you when you're in a hole than find out you were in it later."

"I thought he was my best friend," I say as I fold a pair of trousers over a hanger.

"He's been drunk more than he's been sober. He has to learn

how to be a friend and it's harder to be a friend to someone in pain than it is to someone you just laugh with."

I think about that as we continue to measure inseams and sleeves. I've abandoned friends when it got too hard to help them. I abandon them when it's too hard to help myself.

I tell Jean about these conversations with Kevin after he repeats his peace-patience-gratitude-attitude litany to me a month or more after he'd said it the first time. In the sunniest patches of my routes with the dogs, the roses are frowsy and the hollyhocks are beginning to bloom. I've moved from clothes to books now and have brought over a pile of Tudor history for Ben.

"And just who else is he going to say this to?" Jean asks sharply.

I look up from the table and rearrange their Labrador puppy's face, smooshing her forehead down over her nose and pulling her lips up into a ferocious snarl that still makes her look like the happiest creature on earth. Is Jean taking Jane's side? Bridget grins and clamps her teeth on my arm.

"I'm tired of hearing the same old thing," I say. "I'm tired of not being probed a little for how I'm doing."

"It's the same old thing because you're probably the only one he can say it to. Is he gonna sit down with his sister and say, 'You know how pissed off I always was when you went away for weekends even though I never told you? Well, I'm happy for you now'?"

At the sound of my laugh, Bridget takes a standing leap into my lap and turns to laugh with me. Actually, Bridget is a year old now and is quite a lapful. She is the happiest dog I've ever met and sometimes I turn up here just to love her.

"Of course he repeats himself, Frances. What else is going on in his life?"

"What's going on in mine?" I demand. "I'm depressed. I have to take Klonopin in order to walk dogs. I sleep a lot. I edit. Nothing new ever happens to me either."

"If that's the case, do you really need to say that to him? Say it to me. Say it to Ben. Say it to Jane. You have at least three times as many people to tell how depressed you are and he pretty much has you."

"He has his sponsor."

"Now you're nitpicking. You have a sponsor, too."

Bridget twists in my lap and washes my face and glasses. Damn. I'll have to walk home in a dog spit fog. I hate dog spit fog. I gather her ears together and turn Bridget into Brigitta and sing a bit of "The Lonely Goatherd."

Jane and Jean are right, of course. Maybe it's time to see my sponsor. Maybe it's time to think about the work *I* have to do before Lily moves on to her next stage. While preparing for my death, I've cleared my apartment of a lot of stuff and made room for more of my life. I've saved money to get through the lean days of my dogs going off to Martha's Vineyard and Quogue and Shelter Island, and I've paid off a number of credit cards. I have a new book idea and have been asked for a short story.

I want to care again. I want to look forward to getting up in the morning and working and seeing people. I want to wear earrings and color my hair. I want to want something—Sondheim territory again—and I have a tin box of cash that could pay for a trip to Europe next year if I keep saving. It would be heaps cheaper to go to Amsterdam from New York than from Seattle.

I don't want to move to Seattle in the kind of despair that comes with dependency on one friendship. I don't want to move to Seattle thinking it is the cure for my boredom, writer's block, weight, aloneness, indifference. I know it's not, just as Dar wasn't a cure, or Paul, Galean or Jeremy or any man I ever loved. All of my discomfort in life was there before they broke my heart and it was there after, with a soupçon more doubt and self-blame to add the general scratchiness.

Kevin tells me every third or fourth phone call—which is to say, every three or four months—that he wants to live on the farmette with me. I want to stop worrying that his plans have changed. I want to trust him, trust the silence. It's a skill set to work on, day by day.

I want to trust myself so that if plans change—if I, for instance, decide the relationship is unsatisfying—I'll have the hope and the investment in myself to change with them.

*   *   *

You probably picked up this book expecting a love story or a comedy. I think it is, in the end, a love story that hasn't reached its ending yet.

Maybe it hasn't even advanced very far.

Acknowledgments

The first person I have to thank is my brother Jim Kuffel. He drew a line in the sand about my writing and I did the opposite of his advice, making him responsible for this book and my improved financial ethic.

Bouquets of dahlias to Kenneth and Constance Wilkinson and to Kyra Becker. You are so much a part of my life that my toes would fall off if we were separated.

Bouquets of orchids to my agent, Fredrica Friedman, who kept me on track with this book. A pitcher of margaritas to my editor, Denise Silvestro. There are too many things I need to thank you for, Denise, in the limitations here.

Bouquets of moonflowers to Ann Marie Carley and Gerry Dempsey. You keep me sane.

No woman can live well without a female posse. *Love Sick*'s posse includes Ann Allen-Ryan, Kaylie Beierle, Jennifer Bruno, Marian Cole, Susan Dooha, Jeriyln Hassell Poole, Susan Seidel and Jan Tessier, who have given me the perfect chorus of advice, blunt humor and the needed eye rolls. Constance, Denise and Ann Marie are a part of that chorus as well, in a big way.

And always always always I thank my supporting cast, Daisy and Dad, Leonard Kuffel, my reasons for being alive.